DRUG EDUCATION LIBRARY

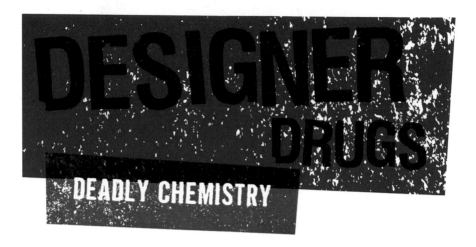

DESIGNER DRUGS

DEADLY CHEMISTRY

By Edna McPhee

Portions of this book originally appeared in *Club Drugs* by Hal Marcovitz.

D0374118

LUCENT
P R E S S

Published in 2017 by
Lucent Press, an Imprint of Greenhaven Publishing, LLC
353 3rd Avenue
Suite 255
New York, NY 10010

Designer: Seth Hughes
Editor: Jennifer Lombardo

Library of Congress Cataloging-in-Publication Data

Names: McPhee, Edna, author.
Title: Designer drugs : deadly chemistry / Edna McPhee.
Description: New York : Lucent Press, [2017] | Series: Drug education library | Includes
  bibliographical references and index.
Identifiers: LCCN 2016052500 (print) | LCCN 2016052896 (ebook) | ISBN 9781534560079
  (library bound) | ISBN 9781534560086 (E-book)
Subjects: LCSH: Designer drugs. | Drug abuse.
Classification: LCC RM316 .M37 2017 (print) | LCC RM316 (ebook) | DDC 615.1/9–dc23
LC record available at https://lccn.loc.gov/2016052500

Printed in the United States of America

CPSIA compliance information: Batch #CW17KL: For further information contact Greenhaven Publishing LLC, New York, New York
at 1-844-317-7404.

Please visit our website, www.greenhavenpublishing.com. For a free color catalog of all our high-quality books, call toll free 1-844-317-7404 or fax 1-844-317-7405.

Contents

The development of drugs and drug use in America is a cultural paradox. On the one hand, strong, potentially dangerous drugs provide people with relief from numerous physical and psychological ailments. Sedatives such as Valium counter the effects of anxiety; steroids treat severe burns, anemia, and some forms of cancer; and morphine provides quick pain relief. On the other hand, many drugs (sedatives, steroids, and morphine among them) are consistently misused or abused. Millions of Americans struggle each year with drug addictions that overpower their ability to think and act rationally. Researchers often link drug abuse to criminal activity, traffic accidents, domestic violence, and suicide.

These harmful effects seem obvious today. Newspaper articles, medical journals, and scientific studies have highlighted the many problems drug use and abuse can cause. Yet, there was a time when many of the drugs now known to be harmful were actually believed to be beneficial. Cocaine, for example, was once hailed as a great cure, used to treat everything from nausea and weakness to colds and asthma. Developed in Europe during the 1880s, cocaine spread quickly to the United States, where manufacturers made it the primary ingredient in such everyday substances as cough medicines, lozenges, and tonics. Likewise, heroin, an opium derivative, became a popular painkiller during the late 19th century. Doctors and patients flocked to American drugstores to buy heroin, which was described as the optimal cure for even the worst coughs and chest pains.

As more people began using these drugs, though, doctors, legislators, and the public at large began to realize that they were more damaging than beneficial. After years of using heroin as a painkiller, for example, patients began asking their doctors for larger and stronger doses. Cocaine users reported dangerous side effects, including hallucinations and wild mood shifts. As a result, the U.S. government initiated more stringent regulation of many powerful and addictive drugs, and in some cases outlawed them entirely.

A drug's legal status is not always indicative of how dangerous it is, however. Some drugs known to have harmful effects can be purchased legally in the United States and elsewhere. Nicotine, a key ingredient in cigarettes, is known to be highly addictive. In an effort to meet their body's demand for nicotine, smokers expose themselves to lung cancer, emphysema, and other life-threatening conditions. Despite these risks, nicotine is legal almost everywhere.

Other drugs that cannot be purchased or sold legally are the subject of much debate regarding their effects on physical and mental health. Marijuana, sometimes described as a gateway drug that leads users to other drugs, cannot legally be used, grown, or sold in half of the United States. However, some research suggests that marijuana is neither addictive nor a gateway drug and that it might actually have a host of health benefits, which has led to its legalization in many states for medical use only. A handful of states also permit it to be used recreationally, but the debate on this matter still rages.

The Drug Education Library examines the paradox of drug use in America by focusing on some of the most commonly used and abused drugs or categories of drugs available today. By objectively discussing the many types of drugs, their intended purposes, their effects (both planned and unplanned), and the controversies surrounding them, the books in this series provide readers with an understanding of the complex role drugs play in American society. Informative sidebars, annotated bibliographies, and lists of organizations to contact add to the text and provide young readers with many opportunities for further discussion and research.

DRUGS BY DESIGN

A growing concern over the last two decades has been the emergence of a class of drugs known as synthetic (man-made) or designer drugs. There is some disagreement over which drugs fall into this category. The term is typically used to describe illegal, man-made chemicals created in a laboratory setting. They are created in the laboratory to produce the same effects as a natural drug, often to get around drug laws: "Legislators would sometimes pass laws prohibiting a substance used in a designer drug only to see a marginally different version appear, using substances not covered in the original law."[1] These new versions are called analogs. Laws have been passed to try to more strictly control the sale of designer drugs. Most recently, the Synthetic Drug Abuse Prevention Act of 2012 made many of the compounds used in the creation of designer drugs illegal. However, drug makers can get around the laws by labeling their product "not for human consumption;" this lets them claim that they did not expect someone to try to eat or smoke the product, and it is often difficult for law enforcement to prove otherwise. They are also sometimes able to make new versions of the drug that are different enough from the old version to be technically legal. Sometimes these drugs are much more dangerous than the ones they are trying to copy.

Other designer drugs are illegal outright, but since they are completely created in a lab, they are still synthetic substances. Designer drugs were initially known as "club drugs" because

The Synthetic Drug Abuse Prevention Act of 2012 outlawed many of the compounds in synthetic cannabinoids, but new ones are being created all the time to get around that law.

they were typically consumed at parties, nightclubs, and large dance events known as raves. In recent years, though, their use has spread beyond the rave scene, and several new, more dangerous drugs have been created.

Who Uses Designer Drugs?

Some of the most common designer drugs include 3,4-methylenedioxymethamphetamine (also known as MDMA or, most commonly, ecstasy); gamma-hydroxybutyrate (GHB), a drug that is often used in date rape assaults; lysergic acid diethylamide (LSD, or acid); synthetic cannabinoids, known as Spice, K2, or "legal weed;" ketamine, a hallucinogenic sedative commonly used by veterinarians; and methamphetamine, commonly called meth.

Designer drug use exploded among young people during the 1990s, but according to the University of Michigan's annual Monitoring the Future study, which charts drug use by students in grades 8, 10, and 12, use of these substances has declined in recent years. For example, the Monitoring the Future study reported that in 2001, more than 9 percent of all high school seniors said they had taken ecstasy during the previous year. By 2015, that number had fallen to 3.6 percent. Lloyd Johnston, principal investigator for the Monitoring the Future study, explained, "Because ecstasy use had been in a pattern of sharp increase in recent years, its turnaround ... and continued decline in all three grades ... were very important developments."[2]

However, while use of MDMA has fallen, the decline recorded in 2015 was not as sharp as the declines reported in previous years. Since 2004, it has fallen by less than half a percent. In other words, while progress has been made toward stopping the drug's use, that progress has slowed. There are still many people willing to use ecstasy, as well as other designer drugs, despite the overwhelming scientific evidence that shows many of them are responsible for dramatic and devastating long-term physical and psychological effects.

A Risky Habit

For years, proponents of hallucinogens—drugs that cause changes in the way people experience reality—have advertised MDMA and LSD as "safe" drugs. They suggest that the drugs are not addictive and that their effects wear off quite quickly. MDMA has even been investigated for possible use in cancer therapy, because it can cause apoptosis (cell death) and has certain anti-lymphoma properties. However, a 2013 review of 25 years of scientific research warned that repeated ingestion of MDMA may also cause deterioration of retrospective memory (memory of things that happened in the past), prospective memory (memory of plans made for the future), problem-solving abilities, and higher cognition (the ability to understand high-level challenges, questions, and concepts).

Most medical professionals, educators, law enforcement officers, and social workers agree that MDMA and other designer drugs are harmful. People have died as a result of using each of these drugs, and they are known to cause many physical and psychological problems.

The date rape drug GHB is particularly dangerous. Because it has almost no taste or odor, a dose can easily be slipped into a soft drink or alcoholic beverage and go undetected. It acts quickly: A man or woman who unknowingly consumes this drug is soon overcome, causing him or her to black out. Additionally, too much GHB can cause an overdose and kill the victim. Women are at a far greater risk of being drugged and assaulted than men, but it does happen to both sexes. Sometimes victims are drugged so they can be robbed rather than assaulted. People who are assaulted while under the influence of these drugs often have little or no memory of what happened. In some cases, a victim may not even realize he or she has been sexually assaulted. As a result, many date rape victims do not go to the hospital until it is too late for physical evidence to be obtained from their bodies. This means it is often difficult to prosecute date rape cases.

Testifying in 2000 before a U.S. Senate panel investigating international narcotics control efforts, Alan I. Leshner, a former director of the National Institute on Drug Abuse (NIDA), warned, "The bottom line on [designer drugs], particularly MDMA, is that given our current knowledge about these drugs, they appear to be extremely risky for anyone's health." NIDA is one group working to find and spread more information on designer drugs. "The citizens of this Nation," Leshner said, "deserve to know what the science is revealing about these drugs."[3]

Chapter One

MUSIC FESTIVALS AND DESIGNER DRUGS

Some designer drugs, particularly MDMA, GHB, and LSD, are used at music festivals, concerts, and all-night dance parties known as raves. Raves used to be secretive, illegal events, but today the only thing illegal about them is the use of illicit drugs, which people take because they believe these drugs enhance the experience. Synthetic cannabinoids and methamphetamine are rarely used at music events; natural marijuana is seen more often, especially in places where it has been legalized. Although drug searches are performed on incoming festival guests, many people have figured out ways to hide their drugs from law enforcement officials.

Rave Culture Meets Drug Culture

Raves were born during the 1980s in European cities, particularly London, as private, after-hours dance parties. The music played at raves has a fast-paced, electric dance beat—the beginnings of a musical genre now known as electronic dance music, or EDM. Eventually, the raves outgrew nightclubs, and parties were staged in vacant warehouses and even remote open fields, sometimes drawing thousands of participants, including many teenagers.

As rave culture spread, so did the use of designer drugs. Certain characteristics of raves encouraged the use of these drugs. Raves are long, sometimes lasting all night. Attendees almost never stop dancing, and it takes enormous energy for dancers to keep up. MDMA became popular at raves because it is a stimulant, which means it keeps its users awake, alert, and active.

Alcohol and drugs such as MDMA are a constant presence at many music festivals; hospitalizations due to adverse side effects are common.

Other observations are described in the book *Up All Night: A Closer Look at Club Drugs and Rave Culture*. Its author, psychotherapist Cynthia Knowles, warned:

The rave experience is an uncontrolled clinical trial of the effects of club drugs on youth. A smorgasbord of drugs is offered for sale to a vulnerable and uneducated population of youth who take these new drugs in combination with other drugs or alcohol. There is danger in the product, danger in the dosing, and danger in the mixing. The long-term effects of the regular use of these drugs won't be known for at least a decade.[4]

DAWN Statistics

According to the U.S. Health and Human Services Department's Drug Abuse Warning Network (DAWN), which charted hospital emergency room visits by drug abusers, in 1994, hospital administrators in the United States reported a relatively small number of overdose cases involving MDMA and GHB—a total of 250 throughout the entire country. Nearly a decade later, however, American emergency rooms reported about 8,000 MDMA, ketamine, and GHB overdoses annually. DAWN also established that designer drugs are primarily used by young people. In 2002, 75 percent of the designer drug-related incidents reported by hospital emergency rooms involved patients age 26 and younger. Unfortunately, DAWN was discontinued in 2011, and there is currently no system in place for gathering accurate hospital statistics.

Drugs are also used together at raves and music festivals. A 2003 DAWN report showed that in the early years of the 21st century, a new trend started making itself clear in emergency rooms: Designer drug abusers were being treated for having taken multiple drugs. According to a U.S. Justice Department report, MDMA is unquestionably the most popular of the designer drugs, but GHB and LSD are also seen often at raves and festivals.

All-Night Parties

Public, ticketed music festivals grew out of the small, semi-secret private raves. The closest relative to raves in terms of atmosphere and culture are multi-day EDM festivals such as Electric Daisy Carnival, Ultra Music Festival, or Electric Zoo. However, the popularity of festivals for every musical genre has skyrocketed in recent years. A recent survey by *Billboard* magazine shows that 32 million people go to at least one U.S. music festival every year.

These festivals draw attendees of all ages, education levels, and lifestyles. However, certain drugs are more popular at certain festivals; in 2015, DrugAbuse.com released a survey of social media posts from festivalgoers which highlighted the popularity of individual narcotics at different events. MDMA is the designer drug of choice at EDM music festivals, possibly due to the need for dancers to keep their energy up for long hours of activity.

Whether it is MDMA, LSD, marijuana, or simply alcohol, drug use at festivals is widespread. In 2015, 77.41 percent of social media posts about Electric Daisy Carnival included references to drug use. The most frequently mentioned drug was MDMA.

One big concern about the use of drugs such as MDMA at festivals is the dangers of the festival environment itself. Ecstasy raises the body temperature; combined with the physical exertion of dancing, this can cause dehydration. Many festivals take place outside during the warmest days of the year, made worse by the large numbers of people whose body heat can be suffocating. Bottled water is generally offered for sale at raves, but at extremely high prices and often alongside alcohol, which can make dehydration worse.

In 2014, the Centers for Disease Control and Prevention (CDC) released a report of "adverse events" (a visit to the emergency room) at a three-day EDM music festival. The report revealed that 95 percent of these adverse events were due to ingestion of drugs or alcohol, the most common being MDMA and similar compounds. Over the course of the festival, 22 people were hospitalized due to substance abuse. Two of them died.

Dancing at EDM festivals and raves can last all night, prompting attendees to take MDMA for energy.

SMUGGLING MDMA

EDM festivals earn MDMA dealers more money than any other type of festival. However, because festivals are now official—and often corporately sponsored—events, most of them have strict zero-tolerance drug policies. In recent years, as the festival scene has exploded in size and popularity, venues have taken extra measures to ensure that the party proceeds drug-free: increased presence of security and drug-sniffing dogs, bag and body checks, policies against open packets of gum and cigarettes (often used to smuggle drugs), and "amnesty boxes" at the festival entrance, where attendees can give up any drugs or illegal substances without the risk of prosecution.

Despite these measures, designer drugs such as MDMA are often smuggled in using all kinds of creative methods and continue to have a large presence at festivals. Many partiers believe that the use of MDMA enhances the festival experience. As Matthew V., a resident of Washington, D.C., told Teen Rehab Center, "Drugs bring your mind to a different place ... You get into the groove of the music."[1]

1. "Drugs at Music Festivals," Teen Rehab Center, August 5, 2016. www.teenrehabcenter.org/resources/drugs-music-festivals/.

Dogs are often used to keep festivalgoers from smuggling drugs onto festival grounds.

Culture and Counterculture

Today's music festivals have become a curious mash of American culture and counterculture. When most people think of counterculture, they think of the 1960s hippie subculture of long hair and bell-bottoms. Many music festivals embrace this comparison: Communal living, harmony with nature, and experimentation with mind-altering drugs are all a part of many festivals. However, some festivals take place in the middle of urban settings, such as Lollapalooza in Chicago, Illinois, where attendees stay in nearby downtown hotels and eat at chain restaurants. Although the experiences are incredibly different, one thing remains the same: MDMA.

Simon Reynolds, author of the book *Generation Ecstasy*, believes MDMA has a lot to do with drawing partiers into a common mindset. He has explained that the drug helps create a feeling of attachment to others: "When large numbers of people took Ecstasy together, the drug catalyzed a strange and wondrous atmosphere of collective intimacy, an electric sense of connection between complete strangers."[5]

In a *TIME* magazine article, a raver named Adrienne explained how the drug made her feel: "I had always been aloof or insecure or snobby, however you want to put it. And I took [ecstasy] and realized, you know what, we're all here; we're all dancing; we're not so different. I allowed myself to get closer to people."[6]

In fact, use of MDMA at raves and music festivals is so widespread that one group of researchers found nearly all the dancers they approached at rave events reported using it at some point in their lives. The researchers' study was conducted by the Pacific Institute for Research and Evaluation, a Maryland-based group that assesses public policy issues.

These researchers interviewed 70 dancers at raves during April and May 2002. At each rave, the interviews were conducted between midnight and 5 a.m, and 85 percent of the dancers that the interviewers approached agreed to answer questions. In fact, the dancers did not hesitate to admit having taken designer drugs and other types of drugs—even though taking them is

Probably the single most famous "hippie" music festival was the first Woodstock Music and Arts Fair, held in 1969. Many people used LSD there, among other drugs.

illegal. After conducting the interviews, the Pacific Institute's researchers recounted that "[86] percent of the respondents reported lifetime ecstasy use [having used the drug at some point in their lives], 51 percent reported 30-day use, and 30 percent reported using ecstasy within the two days preceding the interview."[7]

"It Won't Happen to Me"

Studies indicate that people who do not use designer drugs have a clearer understanding of their dangers. According to the Pacific Institute researchers,

> non-ecstasy users were significantly more likely than past-year users to perceive risks associated with the regular use of alcohol and ecstasy. Not surprisingly, non-ecstasy users were significantly more likely than past-year users to perceive harmful long-term physical and psychological effects associated with ecstasy ingestion.[8]

Others have reported on both the widespread use of MDMA and the lack of concern by users about its dangers. For example, in his book *Rave Culture: An Insider's Overview*, author Jimi Fritz interviewed many users who downplayed the dangers of designer drugs and emphasized their positive experiences. A Canadian raver, who identified himself to Fritz as "J," told the author,

> Ecstasy took me back to a place where I was before adolescence. When the world seemed new and I wasn't limited by my immediate past. It made me think about what I wanted to do and what was important in my life. It reminded me of when I was a child and didn't feel guilty or ashamed or anxious about anything.[9]

This may be an example of what is called "the optimism bias," which is the tendency of the human brain to underestimate the likelihood that negative events will happen. In other words, designer drug users may know and understand the risks of drug

A FATAL COCKTAIL

A troubling trend that has recently been identified is that use of drugs such as LSD and methamphetamine has become more common among users of MDMA. A user at a festival or rave may take a dose of MDMA to enhance the music and the rave environment, then a dose of another drug to achieve a far different type of high. This is known as "stacking" or "cocktailing." "Candy-flipping" is a term to describe mixing the drugs MDMA and LSD. Similarly, "kittyflipping" refers to mixing MDMA with ketamine.

Combining two or more drugs can have fatal consequences. "Stacking increases the risk of overdose, as the stimulant effects of MDMA may mask the sedative effects of alcohol or opiates,"[1] Ellen S. Rome, the head of adolescent medicine at the Cleveland Clinic, warned in the *Cleveland Clinic Journal of Medicine.*

Alcohol, even small amounts, can also be dangerous when combined with MDMA. Alcohol often acts as a diuretic, which means it encourages urination. Mixing alcohol and MDMA prompts the body to rid itself of fluids at a much faster rate than normal. This, combined with MDMA's effect of raising body temperature, puts a partier at high risk for dehydration.

1. Ellen S. Rome, "It's a Rave New World: Rave Culture and Illicit Drug Use in the Young," *Cleveland Clinic Journal of Medicine,* vol. 68, no. 6, June 2001, p. 544.

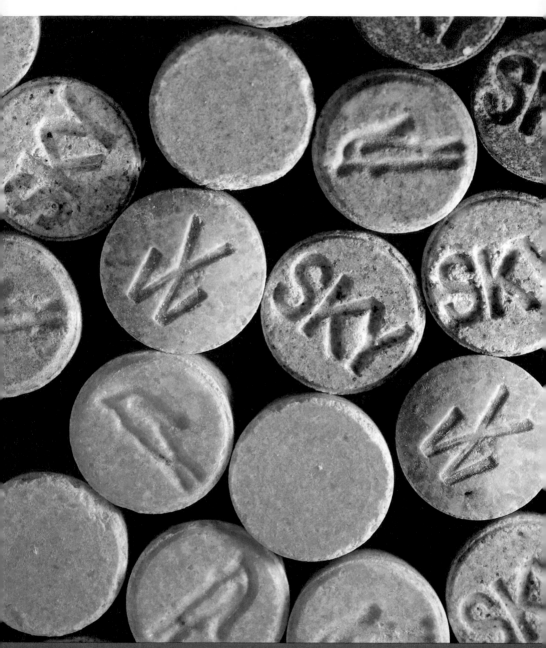

Ecstasy pills often come in bright colors and are stamped with designs, which makes them appear more like candy than drugs. This may contribute to the idea that MDMA is not dangerous.

use, but they use anyway because they believe that adverse events might happen to other people but will not happen to them.

Intended for Legitimate Uses

Designer drugs did not become widely abused substances until relatively recently. Each of the designer drugs was developed decades ago with the intention of using them for medical purposes. However, soon after they were developed, it became apparent that either they had no medical use or the side effects far outweighed any benefits. In the United States, with few exceptions, designer drugs remain illegal substances that are available only through underground channels.

Chapter Two

LEAVING THE LAB:
THE ORIGINS OF DESIGNER DRUGS

Ａll designer drugs were created with the best of intentions, generally with the intention of creating a new medicine or trying to discover more about how the human brain reacts to certain chemicals. As with all problems of substance abuse, the true danger of designer drugs is their use outside of their intended purpose (or, in some cases, their continued use despite being found medically useless). These substances become dangerous once they leave the lab and can no longer be carefully monitored and studied.

Medicinal Molly

MDMA was first developed in 1912 at the German pharmaceutical company Merck. Researchers discovered the substance while searching for a drug that would stop bleeding. Although MDMA did not fit that need, some of the Merck researchers believed MDMA could become useful as an "intermediate" chemical, which means it could be used in research on other drugs that Merck wished to develop.

As its name suggests, 3,4-methylenedioxymethamphetamine is chemically similar to methamphetamine, which today takes the form of the abused drug known as crystal meth. MDMA also contains some of the same chemicals that make up the drug mescaline, a hallucinogenic substance that causes psychedelic "trips" similar to those caused by LSD.

Merck researchers never did find a legitimate use for MDMA, and the drug disappeared for decades. MDMA did not surface again until 1953 when, during the Cold War, the U.S. Army tested a number of experimental drugs, including MDMA, to determine whether they might be effective in extracting

Designer drugs were originally created by professional scientists, but now they are often made in illegal laboratories.

By the early 1980s, some psychiatrists were prescribing MDMA to their patients in order to encourage more open discussions of the patients' feelings.

information from captured spies. In 1969, the U.S. Army declassified the results of its drug tests. According to the army's documents, MDMA was one of eight drugs administered during testing under an army contract with the University of Michigan. The drug was given to rats, mice, guinea pigs, dogs, and monkeys. Another drug administered to animals during the tests was very similar to MDMA—methylenedioxamphetamine, or MDA. MDA and MDMA produce almost the same effects, although MDA causes more hallucinations than MDMA. In the military test, no humans were given MDMA or MDA, but during a separate program at the New York Psychiatric Institute, a large dose of MDA was accidentally given to a human subject, who died as a result.

In 1970, biochemist Alexander Shulgin started a series of experiments with MDMA that included tests on human subjects, including himself. In 1978, Shulgin published the results of his MDMA tests, finding that the drug created "an easily controlled altered state of consciousness with emotional and sensual overtones."[10] Later, Shulgin also declared the drug "could be all things to all people."[11] He suggested MDMA could be put to a number of uses, such as helping people emerge from depression, curing speech impediments, and serving as a recreational substance. By the early 1980s, psychiatrists were prescribing it to their patients to prompt them to talk about their feelings during therapy.

An Overnight Sensation

Around this time, the underground drug culture discovered MDMA. At the time, MDMA was not illegal, so it was sold openly at nightclubs and bars in the Dallas and Fort Worth areas. People could even buy it by calling a toll-free telephone number. During the early 1980s, it was estimated that some 30,000 tablets a month were sold in Texas.

Senator Lloyd Bentsen of Texas soon demanded that the U.S. Drug Enforcement Administration (DEA) investigate whether this popular drug was safe. When federal officials began examining the drug sales, MDMA manufacturers stepped up

Can Ecstasy Help Therapy Patients?

Nearly three decades after he promoted the use of MDMA to treat mental illness, Alexander Shulgin still believes the drug was unfairly banned by the federal government. In his view, the government overreacted to the drug's widespread use at raves. In an interview with Julie Holland, Shulgin said:

Am I happy about where MDMA stands now? No, I am quite sad. Here is a compound [that] when used appropriately ... has the potential of giving pleasure to the user and of being of medical value to those who have certain psychological problems ... And yet, for political and self-serving reasons, the authorities have demonized it and made it a felony to possess and use. In effect, they forbid information about its virtues to be made available. I am proud to have had some hand in uncovering its value, but I am sad to see it become illegal and thus effectively unavailable to those who could benefit from it.[1]

Some therapists agree with Shulgin and are asking the federal government to change MDMA's classification from a Schedule I drug (drugs that are completely illegal) to a Schedule III drug (drugs that can be prescribed by a doctor). These therapists believe that in small doses under a doctor's supervision, MDMA can be helpful because it makes patients more likely to talk about their feelings in therapy sessions.

1. Quoted in Julie Holland, ed., *Ecstasy: The Complete Guide*. Rochester, VT: Park Street Press, 2001, p. 12.

production, anticipating that their operations might get shut down. In 1985, the DEA reported that use of MDMA was widespread in the United States and that research indicated the drug caused brain damage in lab rats. As a result of these findings, on July 1, 1985, the federal government declared MDMA an illegal substance.

During the mid-1980s, the drug began appearing at raves and parties in Europe. It is believed the drug first became popular in the club culture on the Mediterranean island of Ibiza, near Spain. From there, young British tourists who had been vacationing on the island and had discovered MDMA took it to England, where it became popular in London's clubs. A short time later, MDMA crossed the ocean and began to appear at American nightclubs and raves.

In the United States, MDMA was known first as "Adam" and then as "ecstasy." The drug dealer who thought up the name ecstasy admitted that he wanted to make the drug sound alluring, even though the sense of closeness that the drug produced would be described more accurately by another term. "Empathy would be more appropriate," he said, "but how many people know what it means?"[12]

PCP and Ketamine

Decades after MDMA was first produced, during the 1950s, scientists at the Detroit-based drug manufacturer Parke-Davis and Company were searching for an effective anesthetic that would put patients to sleep and dull their pain. In 1956, they developed a drug that seemed to fill both needs: phencyclidine, which became commonly known as PCP.

At first, PCP was regarded as a miracle drug—it was found to be an effective surgical painkiller in very low doses. However, the side effects of PCP soon became evident. The drug caused its users to dissociate, which means they entered deep hallucinations in which they lost touch with reality. PCP often sent its users into uncontrollable and violent rages. The dangers of these rages were made worse by the fact that, because PCP is a painkiller, users do not feel pain when they punch through windows or otherwise injure themselves. Therefore, pain does not cut short the rages, and injured users do not always realize the need for medical attention.

PCP was quickly abandoned, although it became a widely abused drug in the United States because it was cheap and easy for people to produce at home. However, its popularity decreased after the 1980s as cocaine became more common. Parke-Davis still hoped to find a safer form of PCP that would not cause hallucinations or violent outbursts. A breakthrough seemed to have occurred in 1962, when Wayne State University biochemist Calvin Stevens, working in a research program sponsored by Parke-Davis, developed the drug ketamine hydrochloride, which he labeled CI-581. In 1965, Parke-Davis began testing the new drug on humans. Edward F. Domino, the pharmacology professor at the medical school of the University of Michigan who headed the testing program, wrote:

> *None of us shall ever forget the amazing spectrum of clinical pharmacological effects that this agent produced in the volunteers we studied. So unique were these effects that we had to invent a new set of words to describe its anesthetic properties. The drug produced "zombies" who were totally disconnected from their environment, with their eyes open, and yet in a complete anesthetic and analgesic state. The observation of being disconnected from the environment gave rise to the term "dissociative anesthesia."*[13]

Domino and his colleagues believed the drug now known as ketamine could be safe for anesthesia, although Domino noted that the drug's users hallucinated. The researchers recommended that ketamine be administered in very small doses under the strict control of medical professionals. "Since ketamine has some actions clearly related to phencyclidine," Domino explained, "we have tried to find ways to reduce the 'bad effects' of ketamine—or to 'tame the tiger.'"[14]

Parke-Davis received a patent—a license to sell the drug— for ketamine in 1966, and in 1970, the U.S. Food and Drug Administration (FDA) granted permission for the drug to be

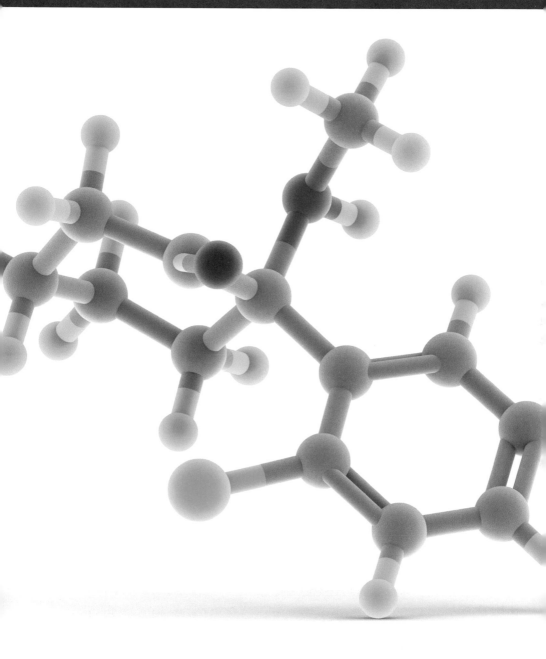

This is what ketamine looks like on a molecular level. It was designed to minimize the uncontrollable rages that its predecessor, PCP, provoked.

used as an anesthetic in both humans and animals. Parke-Davis marketed the drug under the names Ketalar and Ketaject. One of the first places the new drug was employed was on the battlefields of Vietnam, where it was given to wounded soldiers. It was felt that under the small doses recommended by Domino, the dissociative qualities of the drug could be controlled. That proved to be the case. However, as word spread about the drug's hallucinogenic features, it did not take long for ketamine to find its way into the hands of recreational drug users, who took it in quantities large enough to promote hallucinations. The drug was sold illegally as pills; in powder form, so it could be inhaled through the nose or sprinkled on tobacco or marijuana; and in liquid form, so it could be mixed into drinks or injected.

Ketamine on the Streets

One of the first studies of the illegal use of ketamine was performed in the 1970s by Karl Jansen, a former psychiatrist at Maudsley Hospital in London, England. Jansen spoke with a drug user who burglarized a veterinary office and took some of the Ketalar he found there. After injecting the drug, Jansen wrote, the user felt as though he were "floating somewhere above the roof."[15]

In 1978, two books describing firsthand accounts of ketamine use were published. The books—*Journeys into the Bright World* by Marcia Moore and *The Scientist* by John Lilly—describe mind-bending experiences by the authors while they were under the influence of ketamine. Lilly, a doctor, even claimed to have made contact with aliens while under the drug's influence. It has been reported that ketamine, also known as Special K, gives users "a mild, dreamy feeling accompanied by numbness in the extremities [feet and hands], as well as a feeling of being slightly outside one's body. Higher doses produce a hallucinogenic effect and may cause the user to feel very far away from their body."[16]

Ketamine quickly became a well-established part of the illegal drug culture. Because of the danger of abuse, most doctors stopped prescribing the drug, although in recent years, some doctors have begun considering it as a painkiller for the most severe types of pain. In 1999, the drug became a federally controlled substance.

Ketamine is legally used mostly by veterinarians, but even they use it only under certain conditions. Texas veterinarian Wayne Kyle said, "There is no situation where a veterinarian will give ketamine to a pet owner for home treatment of the animal. It is only used in surgery and under strict supervision of the veterinarian."[17]

Date Rape Drugs

Rohypnol is the trade name for flunitrazepam, a synthetic drug manufactured legally outside the United States by the Swiss drug maker Hoffman-LaRoche. The company introduced the drug in 1975 as an anesthetic and as a treatment for insomnia. Rohypnol is in the class of drugs known as benzodiazepines. These are depressants, or tranquilizers, which means they slow the brain and body functions. Rohypnol's effects are similar to those of the widely prescribed tranquilizer Valium, but Rohypnol is 10 times more powerful. By the late 1970s, it had become a commonly abused drug in Europe.

In 1983, the DEA declared Rohypnol a controlled substance. The drug had never been approved for sale in the United States, so American doctors were not allowed to write prescriptions for it. Even if a patient could somehow convince a doctor to write a prescription, pharmacists could not fill it. In 1996, the FDA placed a further limitation on the drug, which made it illegal to import Rohypnol into the United States. However, some drug dealers still sell it. It is most commonly smuggled into the country through the mail. Rohypnol is sold in tablets, although the pills can be crushed and inhaled. It goes by several nicknames, including roofies, roche, and rope.

Some people describe Rohypnol as a "frat drug" or "date rape drug" because in its early history in the United States, it was found mostly at college fraternity parties. When Rohypnol is dissolved in liquid, it does not change the odor or taste of the drink, so someone may not even know he or she has been drugged until it is too late. People who have been drugged

Criticism of fraternities and their relationship to sexual assault and date rape drugs on college campuses has grown loud. Protests such as this one have taken place on campuses throughout the United States, drawing attention to important issues, including the use of date rape drugs.

report not being able to remember anything about their evening 20 to 30 minutes after having a drugged drink. Their friends have reported that around that time, the drugged person begins to act extremely drunk even if he or she has not had much alcohol. If the dosage, or amount of the drug, is very high, the drugged person may become completely unconscious.

Reports surrounding this drug are often confusing. It is impossible to determine how many people are drugged with Rohypnol every year. Many people do not report being drugged, either out of embarrassment or because they are unaware until much later that it happened. By the time they go to the hospital, the drug may have already left their system, so drug tests may not prove anything. Some people believe the media makes being drugged seem much more common than it actually is and that most people who think they were drugged simply had too much to drink; others feel it is an important problem. Without exact numbers and definitive drug tests, it is hard to know for sure.

Although Rohypnol was the most commonly used date rape drug in the 1990s, its use seems to have dropped:

> *One of the pervasive myths about getting drugged is that the drug that is always used is Rohypnol, or roofies, explains Dr. Robert Middleberg, a well-regarded forensic toxicologist and lab director at Pennsylvania-based forensic testing company NMS Labs. Roofies, Middleberg says, are actually extremely rare.*[18]

However, people still use the term "roofied" to refer to being drugged, no matter which drug they were actually given.

GHB is similar to Rohypnol and is also used as a date rape drug. GHB is a naturally occurring hormone in the brain. In 1961, a synthetic version was created as an anesthetic by French biochemist Henri Laborit. During experimentation on the drug, it was found that instead of feeling less pain, patients taking the substance experienced seizures—jerking movements of the legs, arms, and head. It was quickly determined that GHB would not be an effective anesthetic.

In the 1980s, bodybuilders discovered GHB. They saw it as beneficial in promoting the creation of muscle mass and causing weight gain. GHB was sold legally on the shelves of health food stores until authorities started learning of the drug's dangerous side effects. These include:

hallucinations, dizziness … vomiting … memory loss, serious breathing and heart problems, seizures, coma, and death. GHB can be addictive. Long-term use may lead to withdrawal symptoms that are serious enough to require hospitalization.[19]

In 1990, the FDA banned sales of GHB in the United States. In 2000, in response to some 60 deaths reported from GHB use, the DEA declared GHB a controlled substance, giving the government the ability to regulate its use. GHB, which is known on the street as "G," has been found to produce tranquilizing effects much faster than Rohypnol. This is one reason it has been used as a date rape drug. In small quantities, GHB is known to produce feelings of euphoria as well as hallucinations. This makes it a popular drug on the rave scene, where ravers seem unconcerned about or may be unaware of its dangerous side effects. It is also used legally, although rarely, to treat pain from head wounds as well as muscle paralysis in people who have the sleep disorder narcolepsy.

An Accidental Drug

LSD—often simply called acid—was discovered by accident in 1938, when scientist Albert Hofmann was trying to create a medicine from a toxic fungus called ergot. He combined ergot's active ingredient, lysergic acid, with diethylamine to see if the compound would help improve circulation and breathing. Instead of a useful medicine, he created LSD, which did not have the effect he was hoping for. He set it aside, but five years later, he went back to it to see if he could improve it and accidentally ingested some, causing dizziness, feelings of well-being, and hallucinations, some of which were intensely frightening. He tested the drug on animals at a higher dose to

PROBLEMS WITH ROHYPNOL DETECTION

Since Rohypnol first appeared in the United States in the early 1990s, it has become infamous as a date rape drug. Steps have been taken to make it easier for people to identify when their drink has been drugged. The makers of Rohypnol included a dye that turns drinks blue; several companies have invented coasters, cups, and straws that change color when drugs are added to a drink; and a group of college students is developing a nail polish that changes color when it comes in contact with a drugged drink.

There are several problems with these ideas. First, putting Rohypnol in a blue drink hides the blue color. Second, studies have found that the coasters and other test products often do not work well, "changing color for things like different brands of mineral water, taking an extremely long time for ketamine, and giving a false positive once milk was used. Another study ... found that in laboratory conditions, testers only correctly detected two out of three drugged samples."[1]

Third, critics say that these products put the responsibility for avoiding being drugged on the victim, when the blame should actually be placed on the people who try to drug others. Finally, although Rohypnol is the most well-known date rape drug, it seems to have been replaced by other drugs that are easier for people to get. Predators can slip almost any drug into a drink. Xanax, Vicodin, MDMA, and many other drugs are all dangerous when combined with alcohol and cannot be detected with test products. The most commonly reported way of altering a drink is to simply add extra alcohol without telling the victim, so someone will lose track of how much he or she has had to drink.

1. Backdoor Pharmacist, "Date Rape Drug-Detecting Nail Polish Won't Work," ANIMAL, August 26, 2014. animalnewyork.com/2014/date-rape-drug-detecting-nail-polish-wont-work/.

see if LSD was deadly, and although the animals behaved oddly, none of them died. Knowing that LSD would not kill him, Hofmann continued using it and encouraged Sandoz, the pharmaceutical company he worked for, to sell it so doctors could prescribe it to therapy patients.

In 1963, Sandoz stopped making LSD because of concerns about how people were using the drug. Since it was no longer available for sale, people started making it themselves—legally until 1965, illegally after that. Not just anyone can make LSD; it "requires a strong working knowledge of organic chemistry, a complete laboratory setup … and several chemicals that are currently either sales restricted or have their sales closely monitored by the [DEA]."[20] Some of these chemicals can cause cancer, and the ergot fungus itself is extremely dangerous. Therefore, making LSD is a risky process. LSD is most often sold in sheets of blotting paper that "are usually printed with cartoon characters or other colorful graphics. The sheets are perforated into small squares, about a quarter of an inch (6.35 mm) wide. Each square is one dose, and a sheet can contain 900 doses. These squares are chewed and swallowed."[21]

Methamphetamine

For many years, methamphetamine was legal and prescribed for various reasons. In World War II, it was used by the Allies, the Nazis, and the Japanese to keep soldiers awake. After the war, meth was prescribed to members of the general public; it was widely used in asthma inhalers and diet pills in the United States until 1970, when the federal government declared it a Schedule II drug (limited medical use and high potential for abuse and addiction). Amphetamines, which have nearly the same effects but are slightly less dangerous, are sometimes still used in diet pills and attention deficit hyperactivity disorder (ADHD) medicines. Methamphetamine, however, is prescribed very rarely. Large batches intended for sale by drug dealers are often made in Mexico and smuggled into the United States. Small batches can be made by individuals in home labs, but these people are generally making it for themselves, not to sell to others. Because

LSD blotters are often printed with colorful designs.

the cooking process creates crystals that are dissolved in water, it is sometimes called crystal meth. Meth produces a high that makes users feel confident, happy, and energetic, which makes it extremely addictive.

Synthetic Cannabinoids

In the late 1980s, a chemist named John W. Huffman was working with tetrahydrocannabinol (THC), the active ingredient in marijuana. His goal was to figure out how THC reacted with the brain; in order to do this, he and his fellow scientists created synthetic versions of THC. When his research was published, some people realized they could make and use these synthetic cannabinoids to get high. Whether they were aware of the dangerous side effects at the time is unclear, but although the risks are well known now, synthetic cannabinoids continue to be sold.

Synthetic cannabinoids—sometimes known as Spice, K2, fake pot, or legal weed—are sprayed onto plant leaves, and users can then smoke them the same way they smoke weed. However, this type of designer drug is far more dangerous than natural marijuana. Side effects include hallucinations, confusion, extreme paranoia and anxiety, heart attack, kidney failure, and seizures. Although it is not possible to die from an overdose of natural marijuana, it is possible to do so with synthetic cannabinoids. The potential for addiction is also much higher with the synthetic drugs than with natural marijuana.

Dangerous Games

There is a good reason that designer drugs are either banned outright or strictly regulated in the United States. All the drugs can cause both short-term and long-term effects on the brain and body. Some of those effects are irreversible. In MDMA's case, for example, there is evidence suggesting the drug causes permanent brain damage, resulting in "longlasting confusion, depression, and selective impairment of working memory and attention processes"[22] in some people who use it often.

Aside from such negative consequences, most of these drugs also include the very real possibility that just a single dose can prove fatal.

Chapter Three

THE "DESIGN" IN DESIGNER DRUGS

Each of the designer drugs was created in the process of trying to find a medically useful compound; none of them were intended to get people high. GHB and ketamine were developed to put people to sleep, but also resulted in hallucinations. MDMA, a stimulant, was initially created to stem bleeding; the drug failed in that regard. LSD was created in the process of finding a useful medicine to improve circulation and breathing, but it only produced an intense high. Methamphetamine was used to keep people awake and later to help them lose weight, but the dangerous side effects made it unsafe for both of these uses. Synthetic cannabinoids were made in the process of attempting to better understand how the human brain works. These drugs were not developed to be used habitually, and they have significant health consequences for habitual users.

How Do Designer Drugs Work?

Designer drugs are like most narcotics in that they alter the activity of neurotransmitters—chemicals in the brain that deliver messages from cell to cell. Nerve cells throughout the brain and body are known as neurons; each person has millions. Each neuron emits electrical impulses containing messages that control the body's functions. By passing these impulses through the body's network of nerve cells, the neurons work together to tell a foot to take a step, a hand to hold a pencil, or the lips to form words so the person may speak.

Impulses travel along large stems of neurons known as axons to smaller stems known as dendrites. When an impulse reaches the end of an axon, it will jump over a tiny space known as a synapse on its journey to the dendrite of the next neuron. To enable the electrical impulse to make the jump, the neuron releases a neurotransmitter to carry the message. On the end of each neuron's dendrite is a group of molecules known as receptors, which accept specific neurotransmitters and then transmit the impulse to the next synapse. Not all neurotransmitters carry messages, though; some neurotransmitters prevent unwanted messages from passing from neuron to neuron.

Drugs influence the transmission of information in the brain. The drug may produce a flood of neurotransmitters so that too many messages are delivered to the neurons, or it may neutralize the neurotransmitters that work to block unwanted information, causing a flood of unwanted messages to reach the neurons.

The Highest of Highs, the Lowest of Lows

MDMA causes a rush of three neurotransmitters—serotonin, dopamine, and norepinephrine. Serotonin helps regulate mood, sleep, pain, emotion, and appetite. The excess amount of serotonin produced by MDMA causes an elevation in users' moods and is also believed to be responsible for causing hallucinations. "You might feel: a big-time mood lift; an intense bond with anyone you happen to run into; a rush of energy; the urge to talk your head off; or happy hallucinations," wrote Larry Smith in an article about the drug. "Ecstasy triggers a big blast of the brain chemical serotonin, which puts you in a great mood in a hurry. Your inhibitions will disappear and you'll love everything around you, from music to people to plants."[23] LSD also affects serotonin receptors, and it changes the way neurons fire and increases blood flow to the visual cortex (the part of the brain responsible for the way we see things). All of these changes contribute to the feelings of happiness and the hallucinations that LSD users experience.

STRUCTURE OF A TYPICAL CHEMICAL SYNAPSE

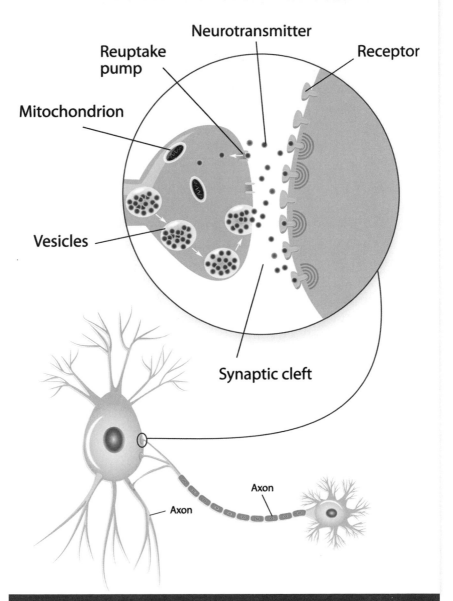

This diagram shows the parts involved in the sending and receiving of neurotransmitters. Drugs can alter this process in damaging ways.

MDMA also causes a surge in the neurotransmitter dopamine, which enables the body to move and also regulates emotions, particularly the feeling of pleasure. Over time, constant and regular surges of dopamine can lead to long-lasting effects. This is because when too much dopamine is released, the brain compensates by permanently reducing the number of dopamine receptors. Methamphetamine also causes an increase in dopamine, and this rush of "feel-good" chemicals is what leads to addiction. Also, since the brain is responding to the stimulation of drugs to create dopamine, the body may make less dopamine on its own. Lack of dopamine contributes to depression. This means that a heavy meth or MDMA user may fall into periods of deep depression when he or she is not using the drug. Meth abusers may also suffer from problems with controlling their movements and moods, as well as issues with understanding written and spoken words.

Because MDMA may cause mentally healthy users to fall into depression, what does it do to people who already suffer from depression? According to David M. McDowell, a former Columbia University psychology professor, the drug may make their existing condition worse. In testimony before the U.S. House Judiciary Committee, McDowell said, "There are numerous case reports of a single dose of MDMA precipitating severe psychiatric illness. MDMA does induce a range of depressive symptoms and anxiety in some individuals, and for that reason, people with depression and anxiety should be specifically cautioned about the dangers of using MDMA."[24]

Finally, MDMA causes a rush of norepinephrine, which enhances feelings of excitement and alertness in the user. As with the other neurotransmitters, norepinephrine's natural production by the body is scaled back during times when the user is not taking MDMA, which therefore intensifies depression between doses. Norepinephrine also controls blood pressure and pulse rate, which explains why MDMA users may find their blood pressure and heart rate skyrocketing while under the influence of the drug.

MDMA's appeal is that it can cause a surge of pleasure, excitement, and joy. However, repeated exposure to it can lead to a permanent shift in the other direction: deep depression.

The Effects of Ketamine and GHB

Ketamine, which has a combination of hallucinogenic, depressant, and stimulant properties, blocks the receptors that accept serotonin, dopamine, and norepinephrine, as well as the neurotransmitter glutamate. Glutamate controls people's feelings of pain as well as memory and their perceptions of the environment. With the flow of glutamate interrupted, ketamine users can find themselves undergoing bizarre hallucinations—they lose touch with reality. Taking a ketamine trip is sometimes called "falling into the K-hole."

GHB may affect the neurotransmitter gamma-aminobutyric acid (or GABA), causing it to bind to brain cells. When GABA binds to a brain cell, it slows down the cell's ability to function. Essentially, this makes people sleepy. In addition, GHB causes a serotonin rush, which elevates the mood of the user and may prompt hallucinations. GHB affects the neurotransmitter acetylcholine as well, which regulates alertness and memory. The release of too much acetylcholine can cause users to lose control of their muscles and even cause them to black out.

The flow of dopamine through the brain is also affected by GHB. Studies have shown the drug both enhances and inhibits this neurotransmitter, which means it can provide the users with either a rush of euphoria or an attack of anxiety.

By consuming ketamine or GHB, the user could fall into a deeply relaxed state, both physically and mentally. That is what makes the drugs so dangerous to date rape victims— they lose the ability to resist or even to know what is going on around them.

Side Effects Include …

All designer drugs produce short-term and long-term side effects on users' brains and bodies. Some of those side effects can be devastating, and in some cases, they are irreversible. The short-term side effects of ketamine can include difficulty breathing and an irregular heartbeat. GHB users may experience drowsiness, nausea, unconsciousness, and difficulty breathing. MDMA's side effects include loss of appetite, decreased motivation, sleepiness, depression, confusion, increased body temperature, convulsions, racing heartbeat, and kidney failure. LSD can cause a "bad trip," where a user experiences very frightening hallucinations and is unable to do anything to stop them. Other side effects include loss of appetite, tremors (shaking), and an inability to tell how much time is passing. Methamphetamine causes both mental side effects—anxiety, paranoia, and mood swings—and physical ones, such as sores and rotting teeth. Synthetic cannabinoids also have both physical and mental side effects; in addition to problems such as kidney damage and seizures, people may display violent behavior, paranoia, and suicidal thoughts.

MDMA may be at its most dangerous at crowded raves because of the possibility that users may become dehydrated. Yet because the drug's effects are not compatible with solitude, few MDMA users are known to take the drug at home or alone. "Ecstasy is above all a social drug," wrote *Generation Ecstasy* author Simon Reynolds. "It's rarely used by a solitary individual, because the feelings it unleashes would have nowhere to go. (A friend of mine, bored, once took some leftover E at home and spent the night kissing the walls and hugging himself.)"[25]

Mental and Physical Dependency

Another danger of designer drugs is that they can be addictive. GHB is considered to be very difficult to quit; a sudden withdrawal from the drug may produce anxiety, insomnia, tremors, and sweating. In the case of MDMA, users eventually build up a tolerance to the drug, which means they require larger doses to achieve the same effect. However, larger doses cause unpleasant side effects, so the experience stops being pleasant at a certain point. Some people feel that this makes MDMA a gateway drug, which means that a user will start taking stronger drugs in order to get the same high. However, researchers are unsure whether this is true or whether MDMA users try other drugs simply because they do not view drug use as a bad thing.

Some drugs create a physical dependency in their users, which means that if a frequent user stops taking drugs, he or she starts

BATH SALTS

Bath salts were first created in France in the 1920s and discarded due to having no medical use. A chemist found and published the formulas online in 2004. The name is actually used to describe several different designer drugs; the most common are 3,4-methylene-dioxypyrovalerone (MDPV) and mephedrone, both of which are synthetic versions of a natural substance from the hallucinogenic khat plant, which grows in eastern Africa. The natural ingredient is called cathinone, so bath salts are officially called synthetic cathinones. Bath salts are illegal in the United States, but people can get around those laws by adding different, legal chemicals to the mix. They were given the name bath salts so dealers could label them "not for human consumption" and pretend they were selling a household product (non-drug bath salts are often used to add color or scent to a bath).

People in the United States first became aware of the bath salt drugs in 2012, when a Miami man named Rudy Eugene was found naked, chewing on the face of another naked man in what became known as a "zombie attack." It was soon discovered that bath salts are highly addictive and produce a high similar to MDMA or cocaine—but with much more violent side effects. These include extreme paranoia, violent behavior, panic attacks, and thoughts of suicide. Sometimes people who take bath salts end up killing or hurting themselves and others.

Synthetic cathinones are generally disguised as household products, such as harmless bath salts, to get around drug laws.

to experience withdrawal symptoms. Most designer drugs are physically addictive, with the exception of LSD. MDMA may not be addictive either; more studies must be done before it is possible to know for sure, although some heavy users do report withdrawal symptoms when they stop taking it. Withdrawal symptoms are similar for most of these drugs and include anxiety, depression, insomnia, tremors, intense cravings for the drug, and more. Many designer drugs also create a psychological dependency in their users. Most users feel as if they need the drug in order to function normally. Psychological dependence can last much longer than physical dependence.

No Going Back

The long-term effects of designer drugs have been documented. MDMA can be dangerous because it causes body temperatures to rise. However, even in cases where use of the drug does not lead to heatstroke, MDMA may still cause permanent brain damage. A 1999 study conducted at Johns Hopkins University showed that frequent MDMA users experience memory loss, and the damage is irreversible. However, as NIDA points out, many MDMA users also take other drugs, so it is difficult to tell whether these effects are from MDMA alone. Additionally, since people are generally studied only after they start taking drugs, it is unknown whether they already had medical conditions that affect memory and mood.

Although some studies have been done on the effects of MDMA, the results are often conflicting. In one case, Dr. George Ricaurte published results stating that MDMA could cause permanent brain damage. Later, he admitted that his research was wrong; he had accidentally given the monkeys he was using as test subjects methamphetamine instead of MDMA.

Methamphetamine has particularly harmful long-term effects, including violence, confusion, and "a number of psychotic features, including paranoia, visual and auditory hallucinations, and delusions (for example, the sensation of insects creeping under the skin)."[26] These symptoms can continue for several

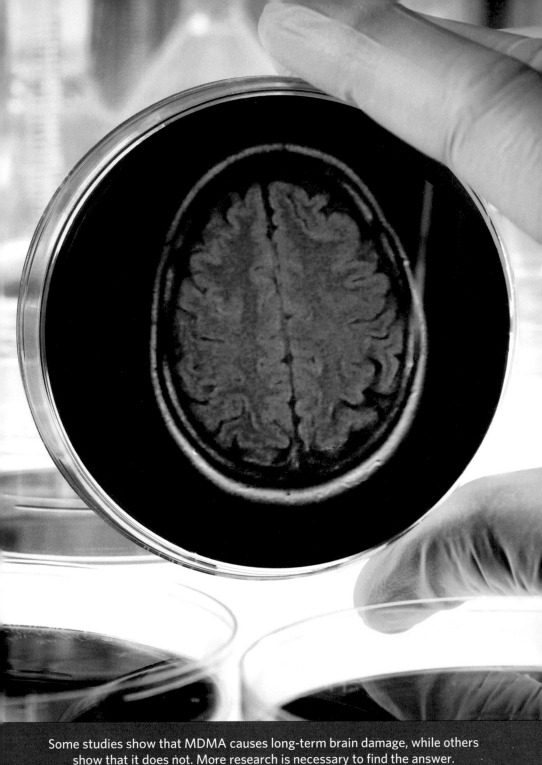

Some studies show that MDMA causes long-term brain damage, while others show that it does not. More research is necessary to find the answer.

years after someone gives up meth, and periods of stress may bring them back after they have seemingly disappeared.

Ketamine also causes damaging long-term side effects, including impaired memory and an inability to think clearly. Users of dissociative hallucinogens such as ketamine have also developed psychiatric illnesses, including depression and psychosis, which means the sufferers lose touch with reality. In cases of psychosis, medical treatment is required to enable them to function in society.

"I'd Heard Nothing Bad Would Happen"

People who take designer drugs risk heatstroke, kidney failure, memory loss, chronic depression, and other physical problems, but much more seriously, they also risk losing their lives. One teenager who died the first time she tried MDMA was Brittney Chambers, a high-school student from Superior, Colorado.

On the evening of February 2, 2001, nearly 40 of Brittney's friends gathered to help her celebrate her 16th birthday. The party was held at the family home, where Brittney's mother, Marcie Chambers, could keep an eye on things. Marcie did not know, however, that Brittney and three of her friends planned to get high on MDMA during the party. "We wanted to experience this together," Brittney's friend Lisa Weaver told *People* magazine. "I'd heard nothing bad would happen."[27]

Just after 10 p.m. that night, Brittney swallowed a tablet of ecstasy. About 90 minutes later, the teenager felt sick to her stomach. Brittney and a friend locked themselves in an upstairs bathroom. When Marcie knocked on the bathroom door around midnight, Brittney replied that everything was fine; she and her friend were just talking. Marcie returned about a half-hour later and demanded to be let in. She found her daughter sitting on the floor, surrounded by empty water bottles. Brittney was disoriented. She slurred her words and seemed unable to focus her eyes. "I knew when I saw her eyes that this was drugs,"[28] Marcie said. She went downstairs and called for the paramedics.

MDMA can make its users thirsty, which prompts them to drink large quantities of water—sometimes too much. That

THIS PRODUCT MAY CONTAIN ...

One of the dangers of designer drugs is that they are manufactured in illegal labs and, as such, may contain toxic additives. Although certain ingredients are necessary to create these drugs, others can be swapped out if they are too difficult or too expensive for an amateur chemist to get. This is known as cutting a drug, and it means someone can never be sure exactly what is in the drugs he or she is taking. A person may take MDMA from one batch and feel fine, then take some from a different batch and become very sick. In 2015, several people in the United Kingdom died after taking MDMA as a result of new types of drugs being added to the mix.

People who make designer drugs (sometimes called "cooks," especially when referring to methamphetamine) do not have to tell anyone what is in their product. Legal drugs are required to go through strict testing processes; illegal drugs are not. Cooks may cut meth "with additives in order to intensify or alter the effects of the drug or so dealers can sell less of the actual drug for more money."[1] People who make LSD may lace it with PCP, which has more dangerous side effects than LSD. Some dealers may not know exactly what is in the product they are selling; others may lie and claim it is safe so people will buy it.

1. "What Is Meth Cut With?" American Addiction Centers. americanaddictioncenters.org/meth-treatment/cut-with/.

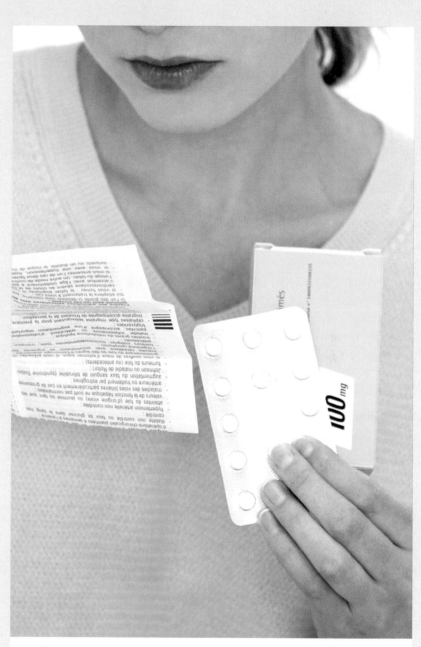

Unlike prescription drugs, illegal drugs do not come with ingredient labels. Many users unknowingly buy drugs that have been laced with toxic additives.

was what happened to Brittney. Shortly after taking the pill, Brittney had felt dehydrated and asked for water. She kept drinking water until she started vomiting. She had consumed so much water that her blood became diluted, which reduced the natural salt levels in her body. This cut off the blood supply to her brain. By the time Brittney arrived at the hospital, she was in a coma. Two days later, doctors told Marcie that her daughter's condition was irreversible. Marcie and her husband, Art Ruiz, stood at Brittney's bedside as she was taken off life-support equipment. "We held her hand and told her how much we loved her and that she was going to heaven," Marcie said. "We told her not to be afraid, that she would be with the angels."[29]

The official cause of Brittney's death was water intoxication. A subsequent police investigation resulted in the arrests of six of Brittney's friends. Marcie Chambers told *People*, "I wish I could blame someone, but the truth is Britt made that choice, she took that pill."[30]

Collateral Damage

Police are well aware of the dangers of designer drugs and have been trying for years to arrest the people responsible for making and selling them. However, it is fairly easy for amateur chemists to change the formulas of some drugs so that every time one ingredient is outlawed, it can be replaced with one that is still technically legal. In the case of drugs that are strictly illegal, such as methamphetamine, the makers can change some of the ingredients in order to keep police guessing about the next place cooks will find their ingredients.

In the meantime, designer drugs remain part of American society, affecting more than just the lives of the people who use them. While those who take designer drugs may suffer from the side effects, others suffer as well, including the friends and family members who must endure the trials of loved ones caught in the cycle of drug abuse. The victims of designer drugs also include innocent people who unknowingly consume date rape drugs, making them easy prey for sexual predators or thieves. Women are targeted far more often, but it can happen to men as well.

Chapter Four

REGRET, ROOFIES, AND RAPE CULTURE

"Rape culture" is a term used to describe the ways that society blames and silences victims of sexual assault while normalizing sexual violence. Designer drugs such as GHB and ketamine have played a large part in this normalization process, particularly on college campuses; Rohypnol (also known as "roofies"), the original date rape drug, became known as "the frat drug" due to its use in cases of sexual violence at college fraternity parties. Although Rohypnol itself is rarely used anymore, the word "roofie" is still used to describe any drug slipped secretly into a drink or the act of drugging someone. Victims who have been roofied do not know that they are taking the drug, and once the effects set in, they are unable to consent to sexual activity and cannot escape their attacker.

Even users who knowingly experiment with designer drugs can experience radical behavior changes, both under the influence and after the drugs wear off. This can lead to actions that users deeply regret.

Dangerous Changes

Many people who abuse designer drugs eventually admit that their dependency caused major changes in their lives. Many find themselves doing things they never thought they would do before they began experimenting with drugs, seeking the pleasurable feelings or the loosening of inhibitions that the drugs cause. Ashley, who used ecstasy during high school, told an interviewer for the PBS documentary *In the Mix* that she often had

DANGEROUS COMPOUNDS

All drugs have side effects, but some are more deadly than others. In the case of designer drugs, the synthetic version of a drug is often more dangerous than the original drug, and when those synthetic versions are further changed, the resulting drug may be riskier still. One such example is called 25I-NBOMe.

This drug, also known as 25I or N-bomb, was created as a technically legal alternative to a less dangerous drug: LSD. LSD has risks associated with its use, but in its pure form—that is, when its makers do not lace it with more dangerous drugs—it has been found not to be addictive, and the risk of overdose or dangerous physical effects is relatively low. In contrast, 25I looks exactly like LSD and creates a similar effect, but with more dangerous physical side effects, including vaso-constriction (narrowing of the blood vessels), which can cause numbness in the hands and feet. Nausea and diarrhea are also effects of taking 25I, and the drug has caused several deaths in the United States, some of those from overdose. Some dealers who sell 25I may call it an "acid substitute" when they sell it, leading buyers to believe it is the same as LSD. Others may also simply tell people it is LSD, which means some people may not be aware of what they are taking.

unprotected sex with boys who got high with her. At one point, she worried whether she could have contracted HIV, the virus that causes AIDS. She said,

You think about it and you're like, "Oh my God ... I had unprotected sex with this guy," you know. I don't know how many girls he's ever been with, what if I got something. I was in that situation and had to go get HIV tested. You can really

do things you wouldn't normally do when you were sober and thinking straight.[31]

Meaghan, another teenager interviewed for *In the Mix*, said that ketamine dominated her life so much that she stole to support her habit. She said:

Just being on K makes you feel like you're drunk, and then being drunk on top of [that] makes you feel like you're just in another world. It's scary. At one point I was spending $300 a week on drugs. I used to steal money from my parents. I would sell anything I could get my hands on.[32]

Michelle, a former MDMA user, told an interviewer for *In the Mix* how ecstasy came to dominate her life:

I'd just sit in my room for like, hours. And I wouldn't leave my room until I was ready to get up and go get high again. Basically, I'd just get depressed and get high to cover that up, and it was just a vicious cycle.

I was a cheerleader when I first went to high school. And then my second year I was barely in school.[33]

Driving While High

In 2000, the U.S. National Highway Traffic Safety Administration examined issues surrounding drug abuse and driving at a conference in Seattle, Washington. The conference was composed of toxicologists—scientists who study the effects of chemicals and other substances on the human body and human performance. The toxicologists studied 16 drugs, both legal and illegal, to determine whether people under the influence of those drugs could safely operate motor vehicles. Among the drugs studied were MDMA and GHB.

The toxicologists concluded that users of designer drugs should not drive. In their report for the Highway Traffic Safety Administration, the toxicologists wrote,

[MDMA] can enhance impulsivity and make it difficult for a person to maintain attention during complex tasks ...

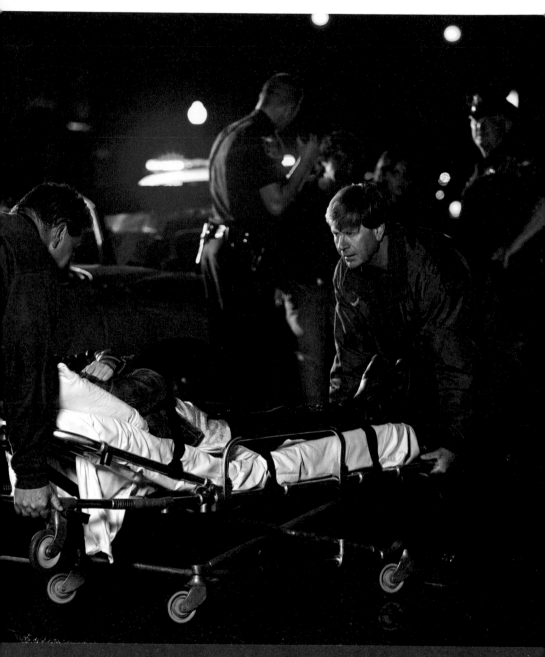

Driving under the influence of drugs is a serious crime and can lead to the deaths of innocent people.

Laboratory studies have demonstrated changes in cognitive, perception, and mental associations, instability, uncoordinated gait, and poor memory recall. Distortion of perception, thinking, and memory, impaired tracking ability, disorientation to time and place, and slow reactions are also known performance effects.[34]

Examining the cases of six MDMA users arrested for driving under the influence, the toxicologists found "the subjects were cooperative and laid back, and experienced muscle twitching, body tremors, perspiring, dilated pupils, slow reaction to light, and poor performance on field sobriety tests."[35] The toxicologists also reviewed arrest records for GHB users. They reported,

The subjects were typically stopped because of erratic driving, such as weaving, ignoring road signs, and near-collisions. Common signs of impairment included confusion and disorientation, incoherent speech, short-term memory loss, dilated pupils, lack of balance and unsteady gait, poor coordination, poor performance of field sobriety tests, copious vomiting, unresponsiveness, somnolence [drowsiness], and loss of consciousness.[36]

Rape, Drugs, and Consent

The qualities of GHB that make it so dangerous on the highway make it equally dangerous to people, most commonly women and girls, who may consume it unknowingly at bars and parties. In this drowsy and dreamy state, people are incapable of consenting to sex and often become victims of rape. During the past two decades, GHB, Rohypnol, and ketamine have all been used as date rape drugs.

The effects of GHB, Rohypnol, and ketamine can begin within 10 minutes of ingestion. The victims lose control of their muscles. Dizziness and sleepiness are common symptoms. The victims may feel the need to lie down. Often, they will fall asleep for 10 or 12 hours and then wake up with no memory of what happened. Very often, they have consumed the drugs without knowing it. While a victim is distracted, someone can slip the drug into his or her drink. Later, once the drug begins to take effect, the attacker can take advantage of the victim's drugged state to commit a sexual assault.

Some victims recall undergoing out-of-body experiences during the rapes; in such a state, a person feels separated from his or her body, like an outside observer of what is happening. These victims realize they are being assaulted but find themselves powerless to fend off their attackers. One sexual assault victim, Jenna, told a writer for *Current Health* magazine that she met a fun and handsome guy named Trevor at a party. After having only two beers, though, Jenna felt dizzy and drunk. When Trevor offered to drive her home, she accepted. At her house, Jenna could hardly stand up and Trevor carried her inside and put her on her bed; the next morning, she woke up sore and

SYNTHETIC OPIOIDS

Opium is a substance that comes from the opium poppy plant and can be used to make many different kinds of drugs and medications, including heroin and the painkiller morphine. Synthetic opioids are designer drugs that have the properties of opium but are created in a lab, just like the other designer drugs. One extremely dangerous synthetic opioid is called fentanyl. It is up to 100 times more powerful than morphine, and although it has legitimate medical use as a painkiller, it is often abused, either on its own or combined with heroin. Some people start taking legally prescribed painkillers as a result of an injury, become addicted, and move on to stronger drugs such as fentanyl when their body develops a tolerance, which means they need more of the drug to get the same effect. Because fentanyl is so strong, it is very easy for people to overdose on it.

An organization called 7000 in Solidarity set up signs in 2015 at the University of California, Los Angeles (UCLA) campus to draw attention to the fact that 1 in 3 women and 1 in 6 men will experience sexual violence over the course of their lifetime. Of 28,000 undergrads at UCLA, that number comes to 7,000 students.

saw her clothes piled on the floor. "Oh no," she thought, "he must have raped me! But how can I prove it? I don't remember anything."[37] Her last memory was of Trevor driving her home. People who believe they may have been victims of sexual assault should go straight to the hospital without showering first. Doctors may be able to collect evidence from a victim's body that can be used against a rapist in court, even if the victim does not remember what happened.

The Burden of Proof

Law enforcement officers are often frustrated in their attempts to track down rapists who gave GHB or other drugs to victims. Sexual assault victims often do not realize they have been assaulted until well after the act—sometimes days. This means that the physical evidence that can be obtained from their body has disappeared or has been washed away. In addition, they often cannot testify in court about the assaults because most victims have no memory of them. Retired New York City police officer John DePresca wrote,

> *How about a case where the victim tells you she knows a crime has been committed against her but can't tell you who did it, where it happened, when it happened, how it happened or why it happened? Every investigator will be called to task when looking into a date rape drug. Rapists now have in their lurid arsenal more than a couple of methods to render their victims helpless.*[38]

In 2000, Gail Abarbanel, founder and director of the Rape Treatment Center at the UCLA Medical Center, Santa Monica, estimated that as many as 20 percent of rapes in the United States are committed by assailants who employed date rape drugs. She said her center first started noticing the use of the drugs in 1995. "Victims were coming in who believed they had been drugged surreptitiously to incapacitate them for the purpose of sexually assaulting them," she wrote in the *National Institute of Justice Journal*.

> *Many of these cases followed a similar pattern. Victims were in what seemed like a comfortable social environment, such as a restaurant, party, or club. Unbeknownst to them, someone slipped a drug into their drink. As they consumed the drink, they began to feel disoriented or sick. The next thing they remembered was waking up hours later, sometimes in a different location.*[39]

According to Abarbanel, when victims first reported the assaults, a common reply from police was, "He has his memory, you don't have yours. There's no evidence. The case is closed."[40] In some cases, police were more sympathetic to the victims and pursued investigations, but without an independent witness—somebody who saw the assailant spike the victim's drink and would be willing to testify—they were often powerless to make an arrest.

Death by GHB

Women who are secretly slipped the drugs in their drinks face the very real possibility of losing their lives because of the substances as well. That is what happened to teenagers Hillory Janean Farias and Samantha Reid. The deaths of the two girls shined the national spotlight on date rape drugs in the 1990s.

Hillory, a 17-year-old from LaPorte, Texas, was a good student and athlete who hoped to win a volleyball scholarship to the University of Texas. In August 1996, just a few weeks before the start of her senior year in high school, she went to a nightclub with some friends. Hillory arrived home at about midnight and told her grandmother she had a headache. She took aspirin and went to bed. The next morning, Hillory's grandmother could not wake her. A police investigation revealed that a soda she had drunk at the nightclub had been spiked with enough GHB to kill her.

Three years later, 15-year-old Samantha Reid of Grosse Ile, Michigan, told her mother she was going to the movies with

Sex with anyone too drunk to give consent is a felony.

Sexual intercourse with anyone incapacitated by drugs or alcohol is rape, whether or not the victim can prove that it happened.

two girlfriends. Instead of going to the movie theater, though, Samantha and her girlfriends visited an apartment to meet four boys they knew from high school. At the apartment, Samantha and one of her friends accepted an offer of soft drinks. After drinking their sodas, both girls lost consciousness.

After a few hours, the boys took the two girls to the emergency room. Samantha's friend was lucky; she slipped into a coma but then recovered. Samantha never woke up, however. The teenagers' drinks had been spiked with GHB. "None of the girls

GHB can be difficult to detect because it is a clear liquid, so it does not change the color of the drink it is added to.

ever knew the substance was put in their drinks," Grosse Ile detective John Szczepaniak told a reporter. "Samantha never knew what happened to her."[41] In the Samantha Reid case, three of the boys who spiked Sammy's drink were convicted on manslaughter (accidental murder) charges and sentences to prison terms of up to fifteen years, while the fourth boy was convicted on lesser charges and sentenced to a prison term of five years.

Fighting Back

The publicity surrounding the deaths of Hillory Farias and Samantha Reid helped increase awareness of the dangers of GHB and other drugs used to facilitate sexual assaults. State and federal lawmakers stepped in, enacting laws with tough penalties for assailants who employ date rape drugs, while police departments underwent training to better understand and respond to the threat. Congress and other federal agencies also have taken steps to decrease the illegal manufacture and importation of the drugs into the United States.

Chapter Five

DEFEATING DESIGNER DRUGS

As the true cost of designer drug abuse has emerged, the U.S. government has increased its measures to prevent and halt the production, sale, and use of designer drugs. Though laws aimed at the protection of victims of sexual assault were the first step, in recent years, laws have increased the penalties for those who use or sell ecstasy, ketamine, and GHB to resemble those for better-known drugs such as crystal methamphetamine.

Congress Cracks Down

The deaths of Hillory Farias and Samantha Reid prompted Congress to pass a law making it illegal to manufacture, distribute, or possess GHB. Adopted in 2000, the Hillory J. Farias and Samantha Reid Date-Rape Drug Prohibition Act made GHB a Schedule I drug, with a penalty of up to 20 years in prison for possession. In addition, the act required the Department of Health and Human Services to track cases of date rape in which drugs have been employed and submit to Congress annual reports summarizing the threat of date rape drugs in American society.

The federal agency was also required to develop a campaign to educate the public as well as law enforcement professionals, teachers, hospital emergency room workers, and others about the symptoms and dangers of date rape drugs. It can be extremely difficult to make arrests in date rape cases, so giving people advice on responding to situations properly is important. In many cases, all the investigators have is the physical evidence left on the victim. Without that, arrests are unlikely, and the extended prison sentences mandated by the tough legislation are pointless.

Congress passed the Hillory J. Farias and Samantha Reid Date-Rape Drug Prohibition Act, which made the penalty for possessing GHB up to 20 years in prison.

Hillory's uncle, Raul Farias, testified before the U.S. House Judiciary Committee when the panel considered the date rape drug law. He told members of the committee,

> *Hillory never drank alcohol, never smoked, and was drug free. The investigation has proved all of this, and ... the one thing that stood out in the investigation, is that Hillory's character was recognized by all that were interviewed. We already knew Hillory was special, but to hear from hundreds of other people, it was just something very special and something very meaningful to the family ...*
>
> *Please put this bill into action. We need to protect our youth; need to protect our daughters, sons, nieces and nephews, and hold people accountable for their actions, especially when it comes to defenseless rape and murder.[42]*

A Profitable Business

What has become clear to law enforcement agencies is that the designer drug trade has been taken over by drug kingpins who rake in millions of dollars. The potential profit that can be made by dealing designer drugs is enormous. According to PBS *Frontline*, "an ounce of meth costs nearly 10 times as much as an ounce of gold."[43]

In 2013, the *New York Post* interviewed an MDMA dealer named Ragan who made "up to $45,000 a month for a couple of hours worth of work a day. Together she and her bosses, Chad ... and Nick ... run a $4 million-a-year operation."[44] Ragan taught SAT classes for $40 per hour but made most of her money by selling MDMA. Chad sold her an ounce at a time—enough to make about 280 pills—for $1,200. She made a profit by selling the pills to customers for two to three times what she paid for them.

The illegal labs that create the drugs also make tremendous profits. Because of the demand for designer drugs, the business has grown from small-time production in homes into an international multibillion-dollar operation controlled by gangs, many

Some drug operations, such as this methamphetamine superlab in the Philippines, are able to create hundreds of pounds of drugs per week.

of them headquartered in foreign countries. The locations of these labs vary depending on the type of drug being made. For example, most methamphetamine is made in Mexico, where restrictions on the ingredients are easier to get around. MDMA is often shipped from the Netherlands to Canada in powder form; the Canadian labs, many of which are controlled by Vietnamese and Chinese gangs, either press the powder into pills and smuggle those across the U.S. border, or sell the powder

The designer drug business is an international, multibillion-dollar industry.

directly to dealers in the United States, who then make their own pills. In powder form, MDMA is called Molly; in pill form, it is known as ecstasy.

The U.S. State Department has been particularly critical of efforts by law enforcement agencies in the Netherlands to find and shut down illegal labs that manufacture ecstasy and other drugs. A 2016 report by the State Department's Bureau of International Narcotics and Law Enforcement Affairs said, "The Netherlands remains an important producer of synthetic drugs, primarily MDMA (ecstasy), of which the majority is believed to be exported … Authorities increasingly find laboratories and dumped chemical waste, especially in the south of the Netherlands."[45] In 2004, proof of the international scope of the illegal ecstasy trade surfaced at Johannesburg International Airport in South Africa, where police seized some 300,000 ecstasy tablets believed to carry a street value of nearly $100 million. The drugs arrived aboard a flight that had originated in the Netherlands.

Protect and Serve

Law enforcement officials have had some success in cracking down on MDMA rings in the United States. Major busts have included a raid on a New York City apartment where police seized ecstasy pills with an estimated street value of $40 million. The two men who were arrested, David Roash and Israel Ashkenazi—both Israeli citizens—were said to be able to supply their customers with 100,000 pills at a time. In 2001, after successfully carrying out an operation known as "Green Clover," local police and federal agents announced they had broken a major ecstasy ring. They arrested 30 people in California and Colorado, including the drug dealer who allegedly supplied ecstasy to the party where Brittney Chambers consumed a fatal dose. Some 85,000 doses of MDMA were seized.

In the fight against methamphetamine and LSD, officials have taken the approach of monitoring the ingredients used to make the drugs and making them more difficult to get. People who buy the chemicals needed to make LSD are watched by the DEA, and in 2005, the Combat Methamphetamine Epidemic

BREAKING BAD

The TV show *Breaking Bad*, which ran from 2008 to 2013, was about Walter White, a high school chemistry teacher who was diagnosed with cancer. Because cooking and selling methamphetamine is so profitable, he used his chemistry knowledge to get into that business in order to pay his medical bills and leave his family with money after his death. The show became a huge success while it was on the air; many people called it the best show on television.

One reason for *Breaking Bad*'s popularity is that it realistically showed the danger and violence of the illegal drug business. Throughout the series, Walter White changed from a normal high school science teacher into a violent criminal. His partner, Jesse Pinkman, was addicted to meth and made a series of bad choices due to this addiction. Walter often found himself in feuds with drug lords, leading to more and more violent behavior as the series progressed. His life changed completely just from being involved in the illegal drug trade, and soon he had damaged his relationships with most of his friends and family members because of his criminal activities.

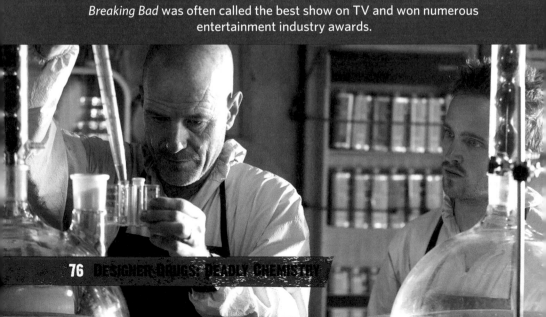

Breaking Bad was often called the best show on TV and won numerous entertainment industry awards.

Act was passed to limit the sale of items such as cough syrup or cold medicine. Most of these medicines have either ephedrine or pseudoephedrine as their main ingredient—chemicals which are also important ingredients in meth. The act required that people show ID when buying these medicines, set a limit on the amount of an ephedrine product someone can buy in one day, and required nonliquid forms of these products to be sold in smaller packages so people would get fewer pills in one package. However, meth cooks can get around these restrictions by paying several other people to buy the ingredients for them.

Officials have also been targeting makers and dealers of synthetic cannabinoids, which have mostly been smuggled from China and widely distributed across the United States. In 2015, a DEA investigation called Project Synergy III led to the arrests of more than 150 people across 16 states. According to CBS News, the investigation "resulted in the seizure of thousands of kilos of synthetic drugs, more than $15 million and dozens of weapons."[46]

As the designer drug trade grows more profitable, it also becomes more dangerous for police officers tasked with shutting down drug rings. Dealers routinely arm themselves for protection. Mark Kleiman, a professor of public policy at UCLA, told *Washington Monthly* magazine, "A street market for an expensive drug is going to be enormously disruptive to the community. This is where MDMA can get scary."[47]

Tom Lowe, the lead ecstasy investigator for the Pennsylvania attorney general's office, told *Washington Monthly* that his job used to require him to work undercover at raves, where he would blend in with the crowd and look for MDMA dealers to bust. Most of the dealers he arrested were young people from comfortable suburban homes who were unaware of the strategies police were using. As a result, Lowe simply approached an ecstasy dealer, offered to buy a tablet, and, when money changed hands, he made the arrest. However, a different investigation took him into a tough neighborhood of York, Pennsylvania, where he closed down an ecstasy ring operated by armed members of the Latin Kings gang. "It's a whole new

Law enforcement officials work hard to bring drug dealers to justice.

ballgame," Lowe told the magazine. "It's not just white suburban ravers anymore."[48]

Do the Crime, Do the Time

While the incredible potential profits may inspire those who manufacture and sell designer drugs, they take enormous risks when they go into the business. If they are caught selling these drugs in the United States, the penalties can be quite severe.

In 1970, Congress passed the U.S. Controlled Substances Act, designating five "schedules" under which all drugs are classified. Schedule I drugs are considered the most dangerous—they have the greatest potential for abuse and have no legitimate medical purpose for the treatment of patients. Illegal distributors of Schedule I drugs face the stiffest criminal penalties. Those found guilty of dealing Schedule I drugs face heavy penalties, depending on the amount of drugs involved and the past criminal record of the drug dealer. On the other end of the spectrum are the Schedule V drugs, which are least likely to be abused and are commonly used for legitimate medical purposes.

Ecstasy, which was labeled a Schedule I drug in 1985, was specifically targeted by lawmakers in 2000. In that year, Congress adopted the Ecstasy Anti-Proliferation Act, which increased penalties for selling the drug. The act raised the minimum sentence for dealing 800 tablets or more of ecstasy from 15 months to 5 years in jail. For selling 8,000 pills or more, the sentence was raised to 10 years.

As for other designer drugs, GHB was designated a Schedule I drug in 2000, making the minimum sentences for distributing the drug similar to the sentences for distributing ecstasy. LSD has been a Schedule I drug since 1970. Methamphetamine is a Schedule II drug because it is very addictive and has a high potential for abuse, but it does have limited medical uses, such as the treatment of ADHD and obesity. The penalties for selling it depend on the amount and whether other types of drugs are mixed into it. Ketamine was made a Schedule III drug in 1999 because it is used by veterinarians as an animal tranquilizer, so it does have a

The penalties for Schedule I and II drugs (as stated by the DEA) depend on how much of a drug is being sold (measured in grams), how pure it is, and whether or not someone has been caught dealing drugs previously.

Federal Trafficking Penalties for Schedules I, II, III, IV, and V (except Marijuana)

Schedule	Substance/Quantity	Penalty	Substance/Quantity	Penalty
II	Cocaine 500-4999 grams mixture	**First Offense:** Not less than 5 yrs. and not more than 40 yrs. If death or serious bodily injury, not less than 20 yrs. or more than life. Fine of not more than $5 million if an individual, $25 million if not an individual.	Cocaine 5 kilograms or more mixture	**First Offense:** Not less than 10 yrs. and not more than life. If death or serious bodily injury, not less than 20 yrs. or more than life. Fine of not more than $10 million if an individual, $50 million if not an individual.
II	Cocaine Base 28-279 grams mixture		Cocaine Base 280 grams or more mixture	
IV	Fentanyl 40-399 grams mixture		Fentanyl 400 grams or more mixture	
I	Fentanyl Analogue 10-99 grams mixture		Fentanyl Analogue 100 grams or more mixture	
I	Heroin 100-999 grams mixture	**Second Offense:** Not less than 10 yrs. and not more than life. If death or serious bodily injury, life imprisonment. Fine of not more than $8 million if an individual, $50 million if not an individual.	Heroin 1 kilogram or more mixture	**Second Offense:** Not less than 20 yrs, and not more than life. If death or serious bodily injury, life imprisonment. Fine of not more than $20 million if an individual, $75 million if not an individual.
I	LSD 1-9 grams mixture		LSD 10 grams or more mixture	
II	Methamphetamine 5-49 grams pure or 50-499 grams mixture		Methamphetamine 50 grams or more pure or 500 grams or more mixture	
II	PCP 10-99 grams pure or 100-999 grams mixture		PCP 100 grams or more pure or 1 kilogram or more mixture	**2 or More Prior Offenses:** Life imprisonment. Fine of not more than $20 million if an individual, $75 million if not an individual.

Substance/Quantity	Penalty
Any Amount Of Other Schedule I & II Substances	**First Offense:** Not more than 20 yrs. If death or serious bodily injury, not less than 20 yrs. or more than life. Fine $1 million if an individual, $5 million if not an individual.
Any Drug Product Containing Gamma Hydroxybutyric Acid	
Flunitrazepam (Schedule IV) 1 Gram	**Second Offense:** Not more than 30 yrs. If death or serious bodily injury, life imprisonment. Fine $2 million if an individual, $10 million if not an individual.
Any Amount Of Other Schedule III Drugs	**First Offense:** Not more than 10 yrs. If death or serious bodily injury, not more than 15 yrs. Fine not more than $500,000 if an individual, $2.5 million if not an individual. **Second Offense:** Not more than 20 yrs. If death or serious injury, not more than 30 yrs. Fine not more than $1 million if an individual, $5 million if not an individual.
Any Amount Of All Other Schedule IV Drugs (other than one gram or more of Flunitrazepam)	**First Offense:** Not more than 5 yrs. Fine not more than $250,000 if an individual, $1 million if not an individual. **Second Offense:** Not more than 10 yrs. Fine not more than $500,000 if an individual, $2 million if other than an individual.
Any Amount Of All Schedule V Drugs	**First Offense:** Not more than 1 yr. Fine not more than $100,000 if an individual, $250,000 if not an individual. **Second Offense:** Not more than 4 yrs. Fine not more than $200,000 if an individual, $500,000 if not an individual.

legitimate medical use. As of 2012, 26 synthetic cannabinoids have been made Schedule I substances, but amateur chemists can change the chemicals in synthetic cannabinoids in order to get around this law.

To fight designer drugs, Congress has passed several laws. For instance, the "RAVE Act," an acronym that stands for Reducing Americans' Vulnerability to Ecstasy, was passed in 2002 and made it illegal for nightclub owners, music festival producers, and rave promoters to allow their properties to be used to promote drug use.

The law was renamed the Illicit Drug Anti-Proliferation Act in 2003. It applied to property owners who knowingly or intentionally allow drug dealing and drug use to occur during parties, raves, concerts, or similar events on their property. The law established civil penalties for violators, which means if they are charged and convicted, they do not face prison time. However, a judge can order violators of the RAVE Act to pay fines as high as $250,000.

Civil liberties groups have protested against the act, claiming it targets a culture rather than a criminal act. Other groups argue that the law ultimately does more harm than good by promoting enforcement and security tactics rather than centering on the safety of attendees through a harm reduction approach. A campaign called Amend the RAVE Act was begun in 2014 by Dede Goldsmith after her daughter Shelley died of drug-related causes: After taking MDMA at an EDM concert, Shelley died of heatstroke. The campaign argues that the law must be amended to reflect the reality that young people will likely continue to experiment with drugs regardless of the risks and legal consequences, so measures must be put in place to make that experimentation as safe as possible.

As Stefanie Jones, the director of audience development for the Drug Policy Alliance, explained:

The RAVE Act—or Illicit Drug Anti-Proliferation Act, its actual name—is legislation that holds event producers criminally and civilly responsible for drug use among their event attendees. Despite almost never being enforced, this law lurks in the background, scaring event producers (and their lawyers and insurers) from allowing anything that acknowledges or even hints at drug use at their events—even information and services designed to keep attendees safe.[49]

The campaign's main concern is that the RAVE Act discourages venues from enacting common sense initiatives that could minimize the risks of MDMA use as much as possible. Goldsmith wrote on the campaign's official website,

DEATH BY DESIGNER DRUG

All drug abuse has danger associated with it, and designer drugs are no exception. Every designer drug has the potential to kill its user; however, the ways in which each drug does this may be different. For instance, it is extremely rare for someone to die from an overdose of MDMA or LSD. An overdose means taking too much of a drug, and since it takes only a small amount of these drugs to create a high, people are unlikely to take enough to kill them. The deaths caused by MDMA are mostly due to heatstroke, hyponatremia (drinking too much water), and taking pills cut with more dangerous drugs. Deaths from LSD are generally caused by a person doing dangerous things while high and being unable to tell his or her hallucinations from reality. In contrast, it is easy to overdose on ketamine, methamphetamine, GHB, or synthetic cannabinoids. It is often difficult for a person to tell how much of a drug is too much for him or her to handle, especially in the case of methamphetamine, which can vary in strength depending on the batch.

Providing free water and air-conditioned rooms, and allow-
ing drug education and other harm reduction services inside
their events would save lives. Yet many event organizers are
afraid that these actions could be seen as encouraging drug
use and therefore subject them to criminal prosecution under
the RAVE Act.[50]

Confronting Addiction

Lawmakers have enacted legislation outlawing designer drugs, and police have used the methods at their disposal to track down and prosecute drug makers and traffickers. However, the drug users themselves must eventually find a way to kick the designer drug habit. Shaking an addiction to designer drugs is often a long and difficult process.

Chapter Six

THE LONG COMEDOWN

Overcoming drug addiction is not just a matter of kicking a habit. Drug dependence affects a user physically as well as psychologically. Often, getting sober means a radical change in lifestyle, from hobbies to friend groups. The saying "once an addict, always an addict" is often true: It is very rare for someone with a drug dependence to be able to reduce his or her drug use to merely recreational or occasional. It is most often all or nothing, and that is a hard step to take when the drug is designed to make users believe they cannot live without it.

The First Step

The first challenge for designer drug users is to admit to themselves that they are addicted. Addiction can be hard to recognize when one is caught up in the middle of it; many addicts claim to be able to stop whenever they want because the drug dependence rationalizes away most of the warning signs. This is why tactics such as familial interventions can be powerful, as they provide the addict with an outside perspective.

In his book *Me Talk Pretty One Day*, author David Sedaris discussed his discovery of methamphetamine—sometimes called speed—in college. He continued taking the drug because he felt it helped him be more creative as an artist, but soon he found that it was controlling his life. He spent most of his money on drugs and had trouble sleeping or functioning without meth. When his drug dealer moved out of town, he used all the money he had available to buy an amount of meth he hoped would last him a full month. Instead, he wrote, "It was gone in ten days, and with it went my ability to do anything but roll on the floor and cry." Describing the withdrawal he went through, he said,

> *Speed's breathtaking high is followed by a crushing, suicidal depression. You're forced to pay tenfold for all the fun you*

Methamphetamine can come in several different forms, including pills, a white powder, or chunks that look like ice crystals.

thought you were having. It's torturous and demeaning, yet all you can think is that you want more. I might have thrown myself out the window, but I lived on the first floor and didn't have the energy to climb the stairs to the roof. Everything ached, and even without the speed I was unable to sleep.[51]

Eventually, Sedaris was able to overcome his addiction, but it was a long, difficult, painful process.

Many organizations focused on helping addicts get and stay sober recommend a 12-step program, which helps break down the recovery process into small steps that can be taken one at a time. The very first of these is for the addict to admit that he or she is an addict. This is often the most difficult step, because addiction can lead to dangerous, harmful, or hurtful behavior for which the addict does not want to accept responsibility.

One of the most difficult aspects of addiction is the way it affects the people surrounding the addict. For this reason, many organizations exist to help the family and close friends cope with the looming presence of a loved one's addiction in their lives, despite not being addicts or users themselves.

Recovery: A Road with Many Pathways

There is no "right" way to get sober. Some people are able to give up their addictions on their own. Others require some drug counseling, but they do not have to be watched constantly. In their cases, outpatient treatment programs can work. The rehabilitating drug users might be asked to meet once or twice a week with drug counselors, who help their clients find ways to change their lifestyles, find employment, or return to school.

It may be necessary for chronic users to enter an inpatient facility. Typically, in such cases, the recovering drug users are expected to remain for 30 days, during which time they are watched constantly to ensure that they do not find ways to obtain their drug of choice. One significant obstacle addicts looking to get sober face is the danger of detoxing, which happens when someone regularly taking drugs stops taking them all at once. In this process, the patient experiences symptoms of withdrawal, which differ depending on the substance but often include sweating,

Organizations such as Narcotics Anonymous and Alcoholics Anonymous use community support to help addicts through recovery.

vomiting, and difficulty focusing. During inpatient treatment, addicts enter a program designed to help them make better decisions once they leave the facility. This program often includes one-on-one drug counseling, group therapy, and strategizing ways to remain sober in the face of temptation.

Throughout all rehabilitation programs, clients are regularly tested for the presence of drugs. Relapses are common, and many counselors consider them a normal part of the recovery process. Very few addicts decide to quit one day and never look back. Sometimes a relapse can help an addict better understand what situations can cause the desire to use drugs (these scenarios are called "triggers").

Bedford Hills, New York, teenager Allegra Miele described her experience in a drug rehab program in an article published in *New York Times Upfront* magazine. She wrote,

> *I was placed in a rehabilitation program. During the month-long rehab, I learned how badly I had been hurting myself. With therapy, I decided that you don't have to prove who you are to anyone but yourself ...*
>
> *I have lost all the friends who used to get high with me. But were they really my friends? Staying friends with them would be detrimental to my recovery ...*
>
> *The hardest part is admitting that you have a problem and that you need help. Once you get past that, you are on the right path. As for me, I feel like I gained my childhood back.*[52]

An important aspect of rehabilitation is removing or managing triggers. Clients are often urged to change their home or social environments if those are spaces where their drug use was enabled or encouraged. Finding new, healthy, positive hobbies and support networks are good ways to minimize an addict's exposure to triggers and lower the likelihood that he or she will relapse.

Not all designer drugs are addictive. According to NIDA, "LSD is not considered an addictive drug because it doesn't

Rehabilitation is a difficult but important process for people struggling with drug addiction.

cause uncontrollable drug-seeking behavior."[53] People may want to do the drug again because they enjoyed its effects, but they typically do not crave it. Although there are no withdrawal symptoms associated with stopping use of LSD, people may experience flashbacks, where hallucinations occur without warning days or months after not using the drug.

In the case of MDMA, studies have not conclusively shown whether it is addictive, although some users report symptoms of withdrawal when they stop taking it. Due to this uncertainty, there is no specific treatment for MDMA addiction. Someone who feels he or she is addicted can seek behavioral therapy from a licensed therapist, but further study is needed to determine how effective this type of therapy is for MDMA addiction.

Stopping Before It Starts

No single factor can predict who will become addicted to designer drugs or when. For some, recreational use of drugs will never lead to dependence; for others, as little as one use can trigger a dangerous switch. Risk for addiction can be influenced by any number of factors, including home and social environment, age, biology, and stage of development. Issues such as gender, ethnicity, and mental illness can contribute, as well as a history of trauma or abuse and even stress.

The only sure way to avoid addiction is to avoid risk-taking behaviors such as consuming designer drugs recreationally. This is particularly important for young adults, whose brains are still developing and susceptible. For this reason, many anti-drug programs target young people in educational campaigns. In 2015, for example, the Partnership for Drug-Free Kids launched a national multimedia campaign that uses emojis to relate to young adults. The campaign, which is called #WeGotYou, features "[i]ndividual emoji sentences ... [that] act as cryptic messages, encouraging teens to 'crack the code' via the unique URL featured at the end of each ad."[54] The ads can be seen on billboards and online, and there is a mobile-only website where young adults can find the answers to these emoji sentences and submit their own.

MOM, DAD, AND DRUGS

Studies have shown that if a person reaches the age of 21 without smoking, using illegal drugs, or abusing alcohol, they are "virtually certain"[1] to never do so, according to the National Center on Addiction and Substance Abuse. Studies have also shown that parents who set clear expectations, and who encourage ongoing, open conversations about defining limits and reasonable consequences are more likely to have a child who does not abuse drugs or alcohol.

Despite this, many parents are unlikely to talk to their children about the dangers of ecstasy, according to a 2003 survey conducted by the Partnership for a Drug-Free America. Of the 1,228 parents surveyed, 92 percent said they were aware of ecstasy, and 90 percent believed the drug to be dangerous. Yet the Partnership found that just 24 percent of parents advised their children to stay away from ecstasy.

Stephen Pasierb, former president and CEO of the Partnership, suggested that parents may not be comfortable talking about ecstasy with their children because they do not understand the drug themselves. As he explained, "They don't truly understand what the drug is, or they truly don't believe their children are at risk."[2]

1. Joseph A. Califano, Jr, "Parents, Massive Public Education Campaign Can Help Save Lives, Money Lost to Substance Abuse," The National Center on Addiction and Substance Abuse, January 8, 2010. www.centeronaddiction.org/newsroom/op-eds/parents-massive-public-education-campaign-can-help-save-lives-money-lost-substance.

2. Partnership for a Drug-Free America, "Survey: Majority of Parents Not Responding to Ecstasy Threat," January 6, 2003, p.1.

The issue becomes even more complicated when discussing date rape drugs, which are often consumed unwillingly and unknowingly. Law enforcement traditionally has urged people, particularly girls and young women, who are the drugs' most frequent victims, to take special caution in situations where there is a risk that GHB or ketamine may be present, such as clubs or parties. Though this is an unfair and undue burden on potential victims of the drugs, it is an unfortunate necessity until a better system for prosecuting and convicting date rapists is found.

Common advice, especially for young women on college campuses, is to never go to parties alone. Friends should watch each other's drinks if they leave for the dance floor or to use the restroom. Also, partiers should avoid drinking beverages from common containers, such as punch bowls, unless they are comfortable with the person who prepared the punch as well as the person who is serving it. People should also watch while their drink is being made or poured to make sure that nothing is slipped in it.

Anyone who suspects that he or she may have been drugged is urged to call police as soon as he or she is capable of dialing the phone. Victims are told to seek medical attention when they are able. Even though the rape may have occurred hours earlier, when the victim arrives at the hospital, medical professionals still may be able to find physical evidence of sexual contact. Victims should not shower before going to the emergency room. If possible, they also should not urinate before they are examined, since they may be asked to provide a urine specimen, which can be analyzed for the presence of date rape drugs.

Victims should save the clothes they wore at the time of the assault and turn them over to police, because the clothes may include physical evidence. If victims still have the glasses that held their drinks, they should turn them over to police as well. Victims should write down all the details of the attack that they can remember. All of these things may provide enough evidence for police to piece together a case and bring charges against the assailant or assailants.

SEXUAL ASSAULT EVIDENCE COLLECTION KIT
CAT. NO. **VEC100**

MEDICAL PERSONNEL
PLEASE PRINT

VICTIM'S NAME: _____

CASE NUMBER: _____

ATTENDING PHYSICAN/NURSE: _____

HOSPITAL/CLINIC: _____

KIT SEALED BY: _____

```
AFFIX
BIOHAZARD
SEAL HERE
```

PLACE SEALED KIT AND CLOTHING BAGS IN SECURE AND REFRIGERATED STORAGE AREA AFTER EVIDENCE COLLECTION

PLACED BY: _____

DATE: _____ TIME: _____ am pm

POLICE PERSONNEL
CHAIN OF POSSESSION

RECEIVED FROM: _____

DATE: _____ TIME: _____ am pm

RECEIVED FROM: _____

DATE: _____ TIME: _____ am pm

RECEIVED FROM: _____

DATE: _____ TIME: _____ am pm

RECEIVED FROM: _____

DATE: _____ TIME: _____ am pm

DELIVER SEALED KIT AND CLOTHING BAGS TO THE CRIME LABORATORY IMMEDIATELY

FORENSIC LABORATORY PERSONNEL

LABORATORY NUMBER: _____

POLICE CASE NUMBER: _____

MANUFACTURED BY **SIRCHIE**® FINGER PRINT LABORATORIES, INC.
100 HUNTER PLACE, YOUNGSVILLE, N.C. 27596 U.S.A.
PHONE: (919) 554-2244, (800) 356-7311• FAX: (919) 554-2266, (800) 899-8181

SEXUAL ASSAULT EVIDENCE COLLECTION KIT

EVIDENCE SEAL HERE

People who have been—or suspect that they have been—victims of sexual assault should go to a hospital, where a rape kit will be administered to collect evidence.

A Different Kind of Drug Test

Each year, music festivals continue to draw hundreds, even thousands, of participants. Some organizations, such as California-based DanceSafe, believe that festivalgoers will continue to use drugs, regardless of the consequences. Rather than trying to stop drug use, these kinds of groups want to ensure that festivalgoers take unadulterated drugs.

MDMA and other designer drugs are dangerous for many reasons, and compounding the danger is the fact that they often are made in unclean environments using industrial chemicals and other harmful products. Also, some illegal manufacturers are known to substitute dangerous look-alike drugs for MDMA. One drug that is commonly sold as ecstasy is in fact paramethoxyamphetamine (PMA), an analog of methamphetamine that is similar to MDMA but has stronger and more dangerous effects. Whereas most of the deaths related to MDMA are connected to dehydration, overhydration, or heatstroke, PMA has been directly connected to several deaths through overdose.

DanceSafe provides music festivals with volunteer technicians who perform quick chemical analyses on drugs to determine their purity. The group claims its quick tests can generally tell whether a raver is taking MDMA or another, possibly more dangerous, drug. However, after the RAVE Act was passed, many venues were worried that having drug-checking technicians at events would cause the venue owners to be seen as promoting drug use, which is in violation of the law. For this reason, DanceSafe also makes and sells drug testing kits on its website so people can do their own tests.

Another company called Bunk Police sells similar kits. One type is the spot test kit, where users can pour a few drops of a formula onto a drug and see how it reacts. Different formulas react in different ways, depending on which drugs are present. Another type is the separation kit. If a user has a pill or powder that he or she knows or suspects has several different kinds of drugs in it, this test will separate out the drugs so they can be tested individually.

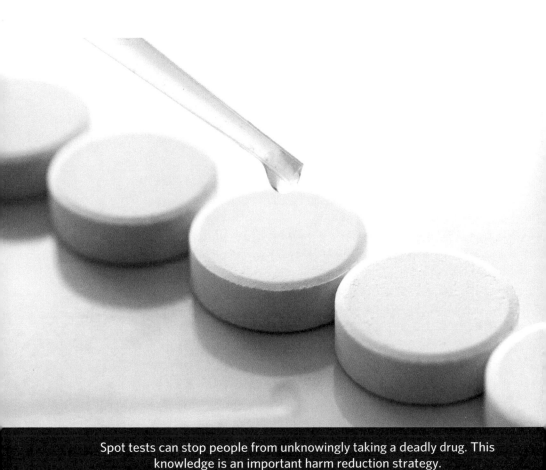

Spot tests can stop people from unknowingly taking a deadly drug. This knowledge is an important harm reduction strategy.

Do No Harm

DanceSafe claims to have saved many ravers from chemical poisoning. Emanuel Sferios, the founder of DanceSafe, called the organization's work a "harm reduction" program and compared it to needle exchange programs for intravenous drug users, which provide addicts with clean needles in order to prevent the spread of diseases such as HIV and hepatitis. He explained,

> [H]arm reduction is an alternative approach to dealing with societal drug use or other criminalized behavior ... It works with people to manage their behavior and minimize the harm that might result. Harm reduction provides an alternative to

DanceSafe encourages festival venues to provide sports drinks for partiers who take MDMA because the drug can cause levels of sodium in the body to drop. Drinks that contain electrolytes reduce the risk of overhydration.

the "abstention only" model. While abstention is the only way to avoid all the harms associated with drug use, many people choose not to abstain. As long as that's the case, regardless of our moral stance on recreational drug use, it presents an immediate need to minimize these harms. Harm reduction programs provide accurate and useful information on drugs, information that drug users can utilize to minimize the risks and the potential harms from their use.[55]

Some police departments have been willing to work with DanceSafe. The DanceSafe technician conducts the test in the open, potentially under the eyes of an undercover drug agent. In some cities, DanceSafe has received agreements from the police not to arrest the dancers who ask for their ecstasy to be tested. DanceSafe also has a set of safety recommendations for festival venues that include "[r]educing ambient temperatures, offering chill rooms, and providing free and easily-accessible water and electrolytes."[56]

Why Take the Risk?

A 2015 study by Monitoring the Future indicates that use of designer drugs is declining among middle and high schoolers. These numbers are lower than they have been historically, but they are still not at zero. This indicates that despite the risks associated with designer drug use, they are still a temptation that can be hard to resist.

People report many different reasons for trying drugs. Sometimes seeing friends or family using drugs can normalize the experience so the risks seem more minimal. Fear of being left out of a shared social experience can also be a powerful motivating factor. Finally, self-medicating for mental illness such as depression or anxiety, for physical discomfort, or to improve athletic performance are commonly reported reasons. However, any short-term boost in mood or athletic performance will often be cancelled out by dangerous long-term consequences.

Notes

Introduction: Drugs By Design

1. John Philip Jenkins, "Designer Drugs," *Encyclopedia Britannica*. www.britannica.com/science/designer-drug.
2. Quoted in "Overall Teen Drug Use Continues Decline; But Use of Inhalants Rises," University of Michigan news releases, December 21, 2014. www.monitoringthefuture.org/pressreleases/04drugpr_complete.pdf.
3. U.S. Senate Caucus on International Narcotics Control, "Statement for the Record by the National Institute on Drug Abuse," 106th Congress, 2nd sesssion, July 25, 2000. archives.drugabuse.gov/Testimony/7-25-00Testimony.html.

Chapter One: Music Festivals and Designer Drugs

4. Cynthia R. Knowles, *Up All Night: A Closer Look at Club Drugs and Rave Culture*. Geneseo, NY: Red House Press, 2001, p. viii.
5. Simon Reynolds, *Generation Ecstasy: Into the World of Techno and Rave Culture*. New York, NY: Routledge, 1999, p. 83.
6. Quoted in John Cloud, "Ecstasy: Happiness Is … a Pill?: The Science: The Lure of Ecstasy," *TIME*, June 5, 2000, p. 63.
7. G.S. Yacoubian Jr. et al., "It's a Rave New World: Estimating the Prevalence and Perceived Harm of Ecstasy and Other Club Drug Use Among Club Rave Attendees," *Journal of Drug Education*, vol. 33, no. 2, 2003. www.ncbi.nlm.nih.gov/pubmed/12929709.
8. Yacoubian et al., "It's a Rave New World."
9. Jimi Fritz, *Rave Culture: An Insider's Overview*. Victoria, British Columbia: Small Fry press, 1999, p. 140.

Chapter Two: Leaving the Lab: The Origins of Designer Drugs

10. Quoted in Julie Holland, ed., *Ecstasy: The Complete Guide*. Rochester, VT: Park Street Press, 2001, p. 12.
11. Quoted in Cloud, "Ecstasy: Happiness Is … a Pill?," p. 65.

12. Quoted in Marsha Rosenbaum and Rick Doblin, "Why MDMA Should Not Have Been Made Illegal," *Studies in Crime, Law and Justice*, vol. 7. Thousand Oaks, CA: SAGE Publications, 1991. www.psychedelic-library.org/rosenbaum.htm.

13. E.F. Domino, P. Chodoff, and D. Corssen, "Pharmacological Effects of C1-581," June 18, 1984. garfield.library.upenn.edu/classics1984/A1984SU44500001.pdf.

14. Domino, Chodoff, and Corssen, "Pharmacological Effects of C1-581."

15. Quoted in Kit Kelly, *The Little Book of Ketamine*. Berkley, CA: Ronin Publishing, 1999, p. 6.

16. "Why Do People Use Ketamine?" TeenHealthFX. December 19, 2013. www.teenhealthfx.com/answers/alcohol-smoking-drugs.detail.html/28574.html.

17. John DePresca, "Date Rape Drugs," *Law and Order*, October 1, 2003, p. 210.

18. Sydney Brownstone, "At Least 10 People Say They've Been Drugged at Seattle Bars This Summer," The Stranger, August 10, 2016. www.thestranger.com/features/2016/08/10/24435013/at-least-10-people-say-theyve-been-drugged-at-seattle-bars-this-summer.

19. "Gamma-Hydroxybutyrate (GHB)," WebMD. www.webmd.com/vitamins-supplements/ingredientmono-950-gamma-hydroxybutyrateghb.aspx?activeingredientid=950&activeingredientname=gamma-hydroxybutyrateghb.

20. Shanna Freeman, "How LSD Works," HowStuffWorks.com, December 10, 2008. science.howstuffworks.com/lsd1.htm.

21. Freeman, "How LSD Works."

22. "What Does MDMA Do to the Brain?" National Institute on Drug Abuse, March 2006. www.drugabuse.gov/publications/research-reports/mdma-ecstasy-abuse/what-does-mdma-do-to-brain.

Chapter Three: The "Design" in Designer Drugs

23. Larry Smith, "Experts Answer Your Top Questions About Ecstasy," *Teen People*, August 1, 2003, p. 240.

24. U.S. House Subcommittee on Crime, House Judiciary Committee, "Recreational Use of Designer Drugs Is Harmful," 106th Congress, 2nd session, June 15, 2000.

25. Reynolds, *Generation Ecstasy*, p. 85.

26. "What Are the Long-term Effects of Methamphetamine Abuse?" National Institute on Drug Abuse, September 2013. www.drugabuse.gov/publications/research-reports/methamphetamine/what-are-long-term-effects-methamphetamine-abuse.

27. Bill Hewitt, Maureen Harrington, and Kate McKenna, "Bitter Pill: One Hit of Ecstasy Killed 16-Year-Old Brittney Chambers Whose Sad Case Fuels a New Antidrug Campaign," *People*, March 4, 2002, p. 52.

28. Hewitt, Harrington, and McKenna, "Bitter Pill," p. 52.

29. Hewitt, Harrington, and McKenna, "Bitter Pill," p. 53.

30. Hewitt, Harrington, and McKenna, "Bitter Pill," p. 53.

Chapter Four: Regret, Roofies, and Rape Culture

31. Quoted in *In the Mix*, PBS, 2001. www.pbs.org/inthemix/ecstasy_index.html.

32. Quoted in *In the Mix*.

33. Quoted in *In the Mix*.

34. U.S. National Highway Traffic Safety Administration, "Drugs and Human Performance Fact Sheets: Methylenedioxymethamphetamine." www.nhtsa.gov/people/injury/research/job185drugs/methylenedioxymethamphetamine.htm.

35. U.S. National Highway Traffic Safety Administration, "Drugs and Human Performance Fact Sheets: Methylenedioxymethamphetamine."

36. U.S. National Highway Traffic Safety Administration, "Drugs and Human Performance Fact Sheets: Gamma-Hydroxybutyrate." www.nhtsa.gov/people/injury/research/job185drugs/gamma-hydroxybutyrate.htm.

37. Quoted in Melissa Abramovitz, "The Knockout Punch of Date Rape Drugs," *Current Health*, March 1, 2001, p. 18.
38. DePresca, "Date Rape Drugs," p. 210.
39. Quoted in Gail Abarbanel, "Learning from Victims," *National Institute of Justice Journal*, April 2000, p. 11.
40. Abarbanel, "Learning from Victims," p. 11.
41. Quoted in Peter Vilburg, "New Highs, New Risks," *New York Times Upfront*, May 5, 2000, p. 10.

Chapter Five: Defeating Designer Drugs

42. U.S. House Judiciary Committee, "Controlled and Uncontrolled Substances Used to Commit Date Rape: Hearing before the Subcommittee on Crime on H.R. 1530," 105th Congress, 2nd session, 1998. commdocs.house.gov/committees/judiciary/hju62309.000/hju62309_0f.htm.
43. "The Meth Epidemic: Frequently Asked Questions," PBS, May 16, 2011. www.pbs.org/wgbh/pages/frontline/meth/faqs/.
44. Madeleine Scinto, "Inside the Lucrative World of Ecstasy Smuggling," *New York Post*, January 27, 2013. nypost.com/2013/01/27/inside-the-lucrative-world-of-ecstasy-smuggling/.
45. U.S. Department of State Bureau of International Narcotics and Law Enforcement Affairs, "Country Report: The Netherlands," 2016. www.state.gov/j/inl/rls/nrcrpt/2016/vol1/253294.htm.
46. "More Than 150 Arrested in Bust of Synthetic Drug Ring," CBS News, October 15, 2015. www.cbsnews.com/news/more-than-150-arrested-in-synthetic-drug ring bust/.
47. Quoted in Benjamin Wallace-Wells, "The Agony of Ecstasy," *Washington Monthly*, May 1, 2003, p. 8.
48. Quoted in Wallace-Wells, "The Agony of Ecstasy," p. 8.
49. Stefanie Jones, "Vice President Biden: Fix Your RAVE Act Law and Save Lives," June 15, 2016. www.drugpolicy.org/blog/vice-president-biden-fix-your-rave-act-law-and-save-lives .
50. Dede Goldsmith, "About the Campaign," Amend the RAVE Act. www.amendtheraveact.org/.

Chapter Six: The Long Comedown

51. David Sedaris, "Twelve Moments in the Life of the Artist," *Me Talk Pretty One Day*. New York, NY: Hachette Book Group, 2000, e-book.

52. Allegra Miele, "How Getting High Almost Killed Me." *New York Times Upfront*, November 22, 2002.

53. "DrugFacts: Hallucinogens," National Institute on Drug Abuse, January 2016. www.drugabuse.gov/publications/drugfacts/hallucinogens.

54. Josie Feliz, "The Partnership for Drug-Free Kids Unveils New Multimedia Youth Campaign Using Emojis to Let Teens Know #WeGotYou," Partnership for Drug-Free Kids, July 7, 2015. www.drugfree.org/newsroom/partnership-drug-free-kids-unveils-new-multimedia-youth-campaign-using-emojis-let-teens-know-wegotyou/.

55. Quoted in Holland, *Ecstasy: The Complete Guide*, p. 170.

56. Emanuel Sferios and Missi Wooldridge, "MDMA-Related Deaths: Stop Calling Them Overdoses," DanceSafe. dancesafe.org/mdma-related-deaths-stop-calling-them-overdoses/.

DanceSafe
800 Grant Street
Suite 110
Denver, CO 80203
(888) 636-2411
www.dancesafe.org
DanceSafe provides volunteer technicians who test ecstasy at raves and similar events to determine the drug's purity level. The organization maintains 15 chapters and affiliated groups in American and Canadian cities.

Drug Enforcement Administration
8701Morrissette Drive
Springfield, VA 22152
(202) 307-1000
www.dea.gov
The U.S. Justice Department's chief antidrug law enforcement agency is charged with investigating the illegal narcotics trade in the United States and helping local police agencies with their antidrug efforts. The agency maintains a number of field offices in the United States and foreign countries.

Multidisciplinary Association for Psychedelic Studies
1115 Mission Street
Santa Cruz, CA 95060
(831) 429-6362
www.maps.org
Founded in 1986 by Harvard University-educated political scientist Rick Doblin, MAPS sponsors scientific research into the use of MDMA as an antidepressant and lobbies Congress and federal agencies to loosen restrictions on the use of the drug.

Narcotics Anonymous
P.O. Box 9999
Van Nuys, CA 91409
(818) 773-9999
www.na.org
Established in the 1950s, Narcotics Anonymous supports thousands
of groups in 139 countries, including the United States. Their week-
ly meetings serve as forums for members to help one another emerge
from their addictions.

National Institute on Drug Abuse
6001 Executive Boulevard
Rockville, MD 20852
(301) 443-1124
www.nida.nih.gov
Part of the National Institutes of Health, NIDA's mission is to help
finance scientific research projects that study addiction trends and
treatment of chronic drug users.

Partnership for a Drug-Free America
352 Park Avenue South
New York, NY 10010
(855) 378-4373
www.drugfree.org
Funded by American corporations, media organizations, health pro-
fessions, and educators, the Partnership helps convince young people
to stay away from drugs.

Books

Bridges, Jay. *Everything You Need to Know About Having an Addictive Personality.* New York, NY: Rosen Publishing Group, 1998.
This book defines addiction and offers tips on how to avoid getting hooked on drugs, alcohol, gambling, and junk food. For teens who already struggle with addiction, the book recommends techniques and resources they might find helpful in kicking their habits.

Eldridge, Alison. *Investigate Club Drugs.* Berkeley Heights, NJ: Enslow Publishers, Inc., 2014.
Ecstasy, GHB, and ketamine are often called club drugs because they are commonly used at raves held at dance clubs. Using them can be risky and may lead to injury or addiction. It is important for anyone interested in attending an event where such drugs may be used to educate themselves about ways to stay safe.

Parks, Peggy J. *Methamphetamine.* San Diego, CA: ReferencePoint Press, Inc., 2015.
The dangers of methamphetamine were not always clear; when it was first developed, it was legally prescribed, and this is still done today in some very rare cases. This volume discusses the history of methamphetamine, the legal and social issues surrounding it, and the different types that can be made.

Scott, Celicia. *New Drugs: Bath Salts, Spice, Salvia, and Designer Drugs.* Broomall, PA: Mason Crest, 2015.
New types of drugs are being developed all the time. Many of them are synthetic versions of drugs that have been around for years. Due to their newness, someone may be offered a drug that they know nothing about. Scott provides readers with valuable information on a variety of new designer drugs.

Torgoff, Martin. *Can't Find My Way Home: America in the Great Stoned Age, 1945-2000.* New York, NY: Simon and Schuster, 2004.
This is a comprehensive history of illegal drug use in America, covering the hippies of the 1960s, disco clubs of the 1970s, and the rave scene of the 1990s.

Websites

ClubDrugs.org
www.clubdrugs.org
> This website, created by the National Institute on Drug Abuse (NIDA), provides information, data on trends, and resources about MDMA (ecstasy), GHB, Rohypnol, and ketamine.

Designer Drug Trends
www.designerdrugtrends.org
> Designer Drug Trends is a yearly report on the state of designer drugs put out by NMS Labs, a group that provides drug testing, professional interpretation, and education.

Drug Facts
www.whitehousedrugpolicy.gov/drugfact/club
> This page, maintained by the White House Office of National Drug Control Policy, provides information about the effects of designer drugs.

NIDA for Teens
www.teens.drugabuse.gov
> This website, also a project of the National Institute on Drug Abuse, is designed specifically for middle and high schoolers who have questions about drug use and abuse, as well as more in-depth looks at the neuroscience of drug use.

Project Know
www.projectknow.com/research/alcohol-and-drugs
> This group provides research on alcohol and different kinds of drugs, including the latest designer drugs. The site gives resources so people who are addicted can find a treatment center near them.

K2, 8, 40
legality of, 6–7, 77, 80–81
risks of, 40, 48, 82
Spice, 8, 40
synthetic cathinones
attacks and, 49
invention of, 49
legality, 50
risks of, 49
Synthetic Drug Abuse Prevention
Act of 2012, 6–7
Szczepaniak, John, 68

T

3,4-methylenedioxymethamphet-
amine (MDMA). *See* ecstasy
(MDMA)
25I-NBOMe, 59
treatment. *See* rehabilitation

U

Up All Night (Knowles), 13
U.S. Controlled Substances Act, 79
See also legislation
U.S. Drug Enforcement Administra-
tion (DEA), 27, 29, 33, 38,
75, 77
U.S. Food and Drug Administration
(FDA), 33, 36

W

Weaver, Lisa, 53

Z

"zombie attack," 49

Picture Credits

Edna McPhee wanted to be an astronaut when she grew up, but when NASA stopped sending people to the moon, she decided to become a writer instead. She has written for a variety of different publications as journalist and short-story writer. She currently lives in the mountains of Colorado with her two dogs, named Tom and Jerry, and an entire room filled with knitting yarn. She still wants to go to the moon.